Hook, Line and Shelter

Ice Fishing Tales and Photos, Too

by
Larry Stark
and
Magnus Berglund

Adventure Publications, Incorporated

Hook, Line and Shelter

Published by Adventure Publications, Inc.
P.O. Box 269, Cambridge, MN 55008

Cover design by Paula Roth
Minneapolis, MN 55402

Book design by
Patricia R. Wagner
Stanchfield, MN 55080

Printed by Sentinel Printing Co.
St. Cloud, MN 56304

First Printing October 1990

ISBN 0-934860-63-7

No Nonsense Disclaimer

Frozen lakes are dangerous even when the ice is two feet thick. Cracks open and close. Underwater springs and inlets keep some spots from freezing up thick enough to walk on. In the northern states a number of people who venture onto the lakes drown, freeze or suffocate every winter. Don't let it happen to you. Stay home and read a no-nonsense ice fishing book.

To Our Parents

Reverend
Magnus Berglund

Violet Berglund

Richard Stark

Noneen Stark

We'd like to acknowledge the help we received from our families and friends and the following folks who spent their valuable time sharing their stories and leads:

Agate Bay Resort
Susan and Frank Anders
Pete Aspen
Mike Averya
Lou Bacigaluupo
Cathleen, Carma and Eben Berglund
Paul and Lenita Bofinger
Craig Brunclik
George and Jerry Chilton
Clarke Historical Library,
 Central Michigan University
Jim Coleman
Chris and Julie Cook
Judy Cornelius
Penny Crandell
Jeff Creuzer
Ron Edinborough
Ron Fisher
Peter and Loreli Genheimer
Hank and Linda Gregoire
Roger and Vicki Gryskiewicz
Ray Hendrickson
Herb Jr. and Carol Hubbell
John and Sue Jahnson
Brother Paul Jasmer, O.S.B.
Jeff, Jerry and Kevin at Jeff's Service
Jack and Linda Jenson
Joe's Sporting Goods

Johnson's Portside Bait Shop
Eric Jylha
Lance and Denise Larsin
Evelyn Leasher
Mike Macalester
Carol Marrin
Jimmy Martin
Lori Rakos Matthews
Gary McIntyre
The Mille Lacs Messenger
Minnesota Department of Natural Resources
Minnesota Historical Society
Ted Natti
Phil Nusbaum
Brad Olson
Jim and Mary Richards
Roger Rucci
Siren Lion's Club
Duane Shodeen
Brandon Shost
Gordon and Gerri Slabaugh
Paul Stanton
Aphrodite, Aaron, Barb,
Isis, Jeanne, Marc and Zeus Stark
Gary Thaler
David and Candy Tripp
Dean and Bonnie Wilson
An anonymous Mille Lacs Lake game warden
And some other anonymous individuals

A special thanks to Richard Stark, Larry's father, for giving us the title "Hook, Line and Shelter."

Photo credits: photos by Larry Stark unless otherwise noted. Back cover photo by Carma Berglund.

Fishin' from the Ford, about 1935. Kenneth Wright, photo, Minnesota Historical Society. Used with permission.

Introduction

It was the year after the invention of corrugated cardboard and in Minnesota an immigrant named Karl Oskar was having an argument with his wife Ingeborg. Finally Karl threw his hands in the air and said, "I vould rather be living in a cardboard box out on the ice there than living here with yew!" Since then, Karl has been called the founding father of ice fishing.

History aside, Larry ventured onto the ice out of curiosity about those little shelters used by people who refused to quit fishing just because the lakes froze. He decided to photograph the structures as architectural curiosities for an art show and to record and to document the stories of the fishermen and women who occupied them. Those first tapes were amazing; we learned about pressure ridges, Rapalas, jigging sticks, and walleye. The stories were better than eelpout.

We quickly learned of the popularity of ice fishing. In Minnesota alone, well over 115,000 permits for ice fishing shelters are issued each year, and that's only part of the story because many fishers don't use shelters. Indeed a seasonal subculture was at hand; a subculture saturated with folklore and packed with exaggeration. We discovered that in the northern states, as the first big freeze closes in and the summer fishermen are throwing a log onto the fire and turning up the TV, the winter ice fishers are checking the line on their rattle wheels, gassing up their power augers, putting in a stock of minnows and hitching their portable fishing houses to their pickup trucks.

We talked to hundreds of people, some fishing in the open, others snug in their shelters. We heard about the right way to set a bobber and the proper method of hooking a minnow. We became connoisseurs of fish house architecture. The shelters we saw were as varied as the terms used to describe them. They were anything from a refrigerator box, tent or a remodeled camper shell to two-story 16x20-foot cabins on runners decked out with fireplace, couch, TV stereo, microwave, carpeting, insulation and Thermopane windows. In our conversations, the shelters were referred to as shanties, cottages, bobs, huts, and shacks. We preferred the term "fishhouse" as one word rather than two to distinguish it from the building where commercial fishermen process their fish.

When it came time to put together everything we had learned about ice fishing, we decided on this collection of mostly-true tales. Like all fish stories they are dramatic, self-serving and nearly metaphoric. They are about real people and real experiences and they take place in a frozen world that is hard for some to imagine.

The picture on the back cover shows both of us hamming it up on the Reverend Roger's front lawn in St. Paul, Minnesota. Bud (Magnus) is on the left; Larry is on the right. Back in the old days, both of us lived on the West Coast where Bud taught photography and writing and Larry perfected his printmaking technique and showed his art in galleries and museums across the country. Larry moved back to the Midwest, and Bud moved to an island in Washington. But we still managed to keep in touch.

In that photograph we're both grinning because it is June and the lure is caught in Larry's shoelace and Roger's lawn mosquitoes are hovering just out of the frame waiting for the last shutter click so they can attack us in earnest. We have already made our annual plans for the coming winter. Lance Larsin has offered to take us out in his fancy house again. Larry says he's going out in his own fishhouse. Bud, now living in California, is not so sure; he is still hemming and hawing and saying maybe next year.

Magnus Berglund
Larry Stark

Take a silo, cut off the bottom, and add some windows and a door and a stove and some benches...

Table of Contents

Beneath this plain exterior lies the Cadillac of fishouses, Lance Larsin's place

Have You Talked to Lance Larsin?

Lance Larsin looks like a blue-eyed hero from a 1940 true adventure comic, clear-eyed and smooth-skinned, a no-nonsense guy. Built like a Norwegian Olympic shot-putter, he's been all over the US and Canada fishing, hunting and camping. When he is not out on a hunting trip with his buddies or outsmarting walleye on a frozen northern lake, he leads a comfortable life in central Minnesota operating heavy equipment.

Larry was out on his road at the mail box when he first heard of Lance Larsin. His neighbor Jim was at the boxes early, too, waiting like Larry for the rural carrier to bring another check that was supposedly in the mail. Jim asked Larry about his current art project and Larry told him about the ice fishing book.

"Ice fishing? There's a guy right here in the county who knows more about ice fishing than any ten other guys you could find. His name is Lance Larsin; he lives right over at School Lake."

Larry made a mental note to call this guy, but, before he got around to it, he found himself at the hospital in Chisago Lakes waiting for his daughter to be diagnosed with what would be mononucleosis. He turned to the person next to him in the waiting room, a deputy sheriff, and asked, "Do you have any ice fishing stories?"

"Sure, but if you want to talk to someone about ice fishing you should look up Lance Larsin. I was fishing in his fishhouse last weekend, and it's incredible."

Larry put a note on his bulletin board, "Call Lance Larsin." It was the week following the hospital incident that Larry had his car at his mechanic's, who told him that the head gasket would have to be replaced before he could drive to Wisconsin. Larry groaned. The mechanic asked why he was going to Wisconsin, and Larry said it was to talk to people about ice fishing. "You don't need to go to Wisconsin," the mechanic said. "You go right here up to School Lake and talk to Lance Larsin. He knows everything you want to know about fishhouses." The two other mechanics in the shop looked up from their work and chimed in, "You bet. You talk to Lance."

Three months later, Larry was driving down Pleasant Valley Road, the back way to Lindstrom, when he saw about fifty fishhouses stored in a farmer's field. The farmer was out sawing up some wood, and Larry stopped. He asked the farmer if he was growing fishhouses, and the farmer said that he just hauled them on and off the ice and stored them in the off-season. He wondered why Larry wanted to know, and Larry told him about the book and the fancy houses he had seen up on Mille Lacs Lake. The farmer looked Larry straight in the eye. "Well, there is one person you should talk to," he said.

"Lance Larsin?"

"Do you already know him?"

"No, but I'm planning to call him real soon."

When we got to Lance's, the fishhouse we came to see was almost hidden from view. In front of it there was a friend's fishhouse tilted up on a trailer. Young basswood trees growing like berry vines covered everything, making it look like a jungle.

"That other house there ain't completed." Lance explained that he had built the frame, but that his friend had built the house all wrong. "It's too high and it has double walls so it's way too heavy. My house here you can get going down the road at seventy miles per hour with no problems. That other thing is too slow. I told him, but he had to do it his way." Lance got the lock off his house and pushed open the door.

What a place. It was all carpeted: the floor, the walls, the ceiling. Lance plopped down on the couch. The top bunk dropped down to be the backrest for the bottom bunk. "All the comforts of home," said Lance. "I've even got the same blankets as on my bed up at the house." Lance smiled like a kid who had just brought the neighbors into his tree fort for the first time. He reached up to the wall beside him to an elaborate electronic control panel with toggle switches, dials and a LED readout. He turned on a circuit breaker and the light over the center table came on, music from a St. Paul radio station filled the room, and the control panel lights blinked on. There was an AM/FM stereo with a cassette deck and an old 8-track deck for Lance's collection of 50s and 60s tapes. "It runs off this breaker that's just like the circuit breaker in your house," Lance said as he flipped one of the switches. The telltale whir of a car's electric window could be heard as the window opposite us went up and down.

We were sitting on one of the wheel wells which Lance explained had been rigged up as a beer cooler with an automatic dispenser. All you had to do was to reach down to the end of the delivery tunnel and a cold beer would fall into your hand. At the end of a fishing trip, the lid could be opened and the fish stored there for the ride home. Lance sat on the couch at the end of the trailer/house. There were arm rests with dowel pins that pushed right into the walls. Across from us was the other wheel well and another covered beer cooler. At the front of the trailer was the TV, the hidden stove, and the empty aquarium tank.

"There's really going to be an aquarium in it?" we asked.

"You bet it's going to have an aquarium; it will have lights run from the panel board along with everything else. It's all hooked up with computer chips. You can turn on everything in the fishhouse and only draw an amp and a half of power. When you have a hundred-amp battery, it lasts quite awhile. Every time I hook it up to the car or pickup, I plug in my welding leads, and it's just like having two batteries, one on the fishhouse fender and one on the truck fender. The minute I go down the road it automatically gets charged up."

Outside was the trailer hitch and a fake chimney covered with red brick-patterned siding. We told Lance that from the outside it really looked like the house had a fireplace. He said, "All that is, is a place to put all the stuff in the wall, like the cook stove." He rolled his cook stove out of a drawer-sized opening next to the hundred-pound LP gas cylinder under the empty aquarium. A couple of drawers took care of the cooking pans and utensils. "There is also the TV here. Over on this side is a shelf for your fishing gear."

In the center of the one-room trailer was a glass-covered round table supported by one post in the middle that was built like a hat rack for liquor bottles. You could see through the table top to the bottle you wanted. Above the table was the light that could be pulled down close to the table for some serious card playing or left up high to illuminate the entire room.

Lance had installed electric cigarette lighters in the walls by each seat. He planned on putting a stainless steel plate around each lighter so the carpeting didn't get burned. Since neither he nor his friends smoked, we asked him why he put the lighters in. "It's where I plug in the electric hole auger," he said.

Sitting there in his house in the basswood trees it was easy to forget that it had been designed for winter fishing. You wouldn't have guessed there were four fishing holes cut in the floor. Closed, the carpet-backed trap doors matched perfectly with the rest of the floor. Each trap door had a small motor controlled through the panel. This way Lance could open the covers from the couch.

We asked if the fishing lines were dropped by remote control from the power panel and he said, "It can be done, but no, not yet." Lance went on to explain how the panel worked. "It tells you when you have a fish. Each hole has a number: One, two, three, four. If a fish bites, say on the line in hole number three, the line goes through these points, and it sets off the alarm. Then the digital readout will display a blinking '3.'

"Say you're sleeping, and the alarm goes off. You get up and go right to hole number three. When you get to the hole you turn on the light above the hole. After you take the fish off the line, you reset the line through the electrical points, and the light on the control panel goes off."

Lance also had his alarm system rigged up to the outside. A little red beacon light on the end of a piece of conduit stuck up above the doorway. Lance said, "Say you're outside cutting holes or you're at your neighbor's drinking beer. You get a fish and the alarm goes off, but you can't hear it, so then what? The light goes on outside on the top of the fishhouse. Now you don't want everybody and his brother to know that you have a fish, see? If I'm at my buddy's house, I sit in a position so I can see my house, and if the light goes on, then instead of saying, 'I got a fish on,' and I get six guys stuck in the doorway, I just say, 'Well, I gotta take a leak,' step outside the doorway, and make a mad dash to take the fish off."

We asked Lance how long it took him to build this house on wheels. He said, "It's not done yet. Actually what happened was I bet a guy I'd have it done in thirty days. He bet me two cases of beer. I had ten days left, and all I had to do was put in the motorized outfit to open up the holes, box in the fireplace, put the aquarium in the wall, put the solar heat on it, and it would have been finished good enough so that I could have collected my two cases of beer. But then we got drinking up town, and I said, 'I'll tell you what I'm going to do. I'm going to let you off the hook.' It was pretty near Christmas, and I said, 'If you bring a case of beer over tomorrow while I'm working on the fishhouse, I'll let you off the hook.' So the next day, here he comes. I just dropped the wrenches right there, and we took it to sea. I haven't done a shittin' thing to it for the six months since."

On the wall across from us between the beer cooler and the front corner fish hole was the trash opening. Lance said, "This stainless square is where your empty whiskey bottles and other trash go. There is a butterfly on it so all the trash goes right outside the house and into a trash can tied to the side. When you get ready to move you take it off and put it inside."

One of his slickest inventions can only be appreciated by someone who has set up a fishhouse on the ice and then had it freeze to the lake. Lance can set his trailer bed right down on the ice and then pop it up whenever he is ready to hit the road, all without lifting more than a finger to the control panel. The whole thing works like the landing gear on an airplane: push the button and the wheels tuck up inside the wells and the frame settles onto the ice. Press it again and it comes right back up ready to hook up and drive away.

"You can't beat this. I've been in a lot of houses and you can't beat this one for fishing. I've got a V-plow on the truck wide enough so that I can drive out on the lake, push the snow out of the way, open the door and drill a hole while I'm sitting in the truck. When I'm up north, I just mount the auger to the power take-off on the front of the truck and drill holes as I go along.

"I know just about where the reefs and bars are so I just go along and drill holes every fifteen or twenty feet and check them. When I get to the drop-offs where the sand ends, that's where I want to fish. A lot of guys will use depth finders, but I use a lead weight on a line. That way I know what kind of bottom is there by how the weight feels when it hits.

"Sometimes I'll hit three lakes in one day. You just hit the button and you're gone. And you got the electric auger to use in the house too so there's no smoke. You plug it into one of those cigarette lighters, and it drills a seven-inch hole. I also have a gas auger for my outside test holes."

We were beginning to wonder if Lance ever did any serious fishing or if he was just wrapped up in his eccentric technology. When he opened a picture album and started showing us his pictures, the fish were lined up from edge to edge in every shot.

"I tell you," Lance continued, "last year I caught the nicest bunch of walleyes that I've caught in four years now. I went to a place where I've never seen anybody else fish and I've been up here since 1954.

"The lake has mud flats at about twelve to fourteen feet deep, and I'm looking for a good spot for walleye, something around twelve to eighteen feet. I went out there and plowed out an area with the V-plow and drilled a hole and the water was seventeen feet deep. I thought I'd just fish there that night. I drilled two holes in the house and put my orange lead-weight depth-finder down. It got down about two feet and disappeared. The water was so dirty and milky that you couldn't see anything, but I put a minnow down anyway for the heck of it.

"It was about five o'clock, prime time fishing, but after fifteen or twenty minutes I knew I wasn't going to get any fish and I did the most unorthodox thing I've ever done. I just left the line in. I went away and just left the line in the water."

Lance laughed. He was leaning forward on the couch. He had us like a couple of fish and he was playing us now. We were the tenderfeet listening to the old-timer spinning yarns, wondering where the edge was between truth and fiction; we were caught and enjoying every minute of it.

"So, there I was with that line in the water, and I came back in the morning and the line was all run out and going *ting, ting, ting*. I thought at first it was a jack. You know those northern will run in spurts, but then I saw that it was pulling like a walleye. I knew something was on it and I pulled in an eight-pound walleye. I had planned to pull out of there, but I decided to put the line down again

and go outside to drill another hole. I didn't even get the second line
down, and the first one started to go. I got a six-pounder, and it just
went that way until the end of the season. I caught fish after fish after
fish. I was giving them away like I was crazy and fishing with nobody
around me. Everybody was wondering where I was fishing, and they
were sending out scouting parties trying to find me, but nobody
could."

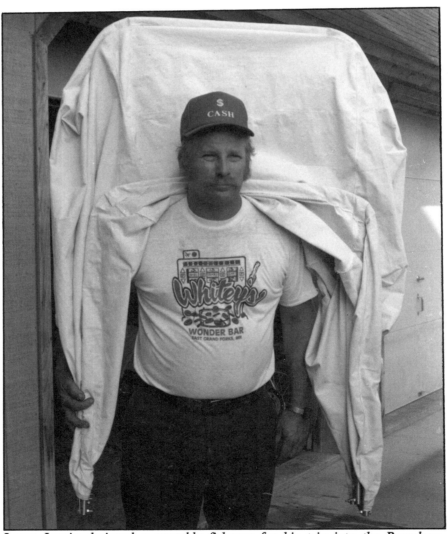

*Lance Larsin designed a portable fishouse for his trip into the Boundary
Waters Canoe Area. It folds up and fits on top of his backpack/fishing chair.*

The House with Eight Holes

There once was a fishouse with eight holes. It was off by itself away on its own little bay atop its own little reef on its own little part of the lake. Inside, there was a fisherman who caught lots of fish. He caught perch, crappies and walleye. There was also a warden who visited this lake and who knew about the little house that was off by itself. Each time he visited the little house he noticed that the fisherman had only two lines in the water which was the legal limit for this area. He also noticed two other important facts: the fisherman had eight holes augured open even though he fished alone, and the fishouse had windows on all four sides so that an officer of the law could not approach without being seen.

For several years, the game warden was preoccupied with the house with eight holes. He was sure that the fisherman was fishing all eight. The warden began to see the house with eight holes as his mission. He thought about it when he got up in the morning. He could not think about fishing without thinking about the smugness of the fisherman off on his own little part of the lake looking out of his windows.

The fisherman felt safe. He had built his fort so he could scan the horizon. He was confident that no one could surprise him. There was nothing to see but bare ice, snow and trees.

The warden was a clever man. He was not going to be tricked by any fisherman. He began to think about Trojan horses. He thought about the criminal mind, smugness and overconfidence. He was forming a plan.

In the fishouse all eight holes were augured open, but the fisherman pretended to use only two at a time. He was confident that he could get the lines out of the extra holes in the event the warden knocked at his door. Meanwhile, the warden was building a little smugness of his own.

One day a new fishouse appeared near the one with eight holes. It was not too close, but it made the fisherman uneasy. It was too late in the season to think of moving his house and re-drilling his eight holes so he stayed where he was, but he did not feel as smug as he had before.

The warden sat in his truck at the side of the lake and watched through his binoculars. He had figured that the fisherman would not move his house, and he was glad to see he was right. Each day he watched from the truck. He wanted the fisherman to become used to the new fishouse.

When the warden had waited the time that only a warden can wait, he drove to a place far from the house with eight holes. It could not be seen by the fisherman because of the new fishhouse. The warden got on his snowmobile. He put on his sunglasses and drove quickly across the ice to the new fishhouse, where he waited again.

The warden knew that the fisherman had heard him, but he hoped he had not seen him and that he would forget about what he had heard and go back to tending his eight fishing holes. People believe what they want to believe, and one bit of noise in an otherwise peaceful landscape was not going to change the fisherman's perception of reality. The warden turned off the engine and sat there on the snowmobile on the far side of the new house. He waited longer than a warden can wait and then he waited some more. He knew this trick would work only once.

When the time was right, he started the snowmobile and sped across the ice to the house with eight holes. He jumped off and yanked open the door.

The fisherman had been sitting on his Port-a-Potty when he heard the snowmobile come from behind the new fishhouse. He jumped up and, with his pants around his shoes, started pulling fish lines out of all eight holes. The fisherman was caught. The warden was mooned. The fisherman was quick to give up. "I don't suppose you're here to see my license."

Getting Away from the Wife

Roger was another ice fishing resource whom Larry discovered close to home. He was a math teacher at a local high school and, since some of his students had trouble pronouncing his last name, they called him Mr. Z.
Larry tells this story.

It took me a while to get into this ice fishing project. At first I was happy to photograph fishouses from a distance. Then I started talking to people about what they were really doing out there on the ice and I soon began to ask everyone I met if they had ever been ice fishing; I talked to people at gas stations, banks, and supermarkets. My youngest daughter had watched this whole process with the cool eye of a budding journalist, and one day she said that I should talk to Mr. Z who went ice fishing to get away from his wife. I asked her how she knew he went for that reason.

"He told us in class."

Mr. Z agreed to talk to me, but only if I would fish with him. No problem. I was anxious to get out on the ice and see the inside of his fishouse.

We drove out together from the town of Forest Lake to the lake with the same name. His fishouse turned out to be about the same size as most of the ones that I had photographed so far. If it weren't for the slightly pitched roof, it would have been a perfect eight-foot plywood cube. It kept him dry, gave him some privacy, and it kept the cold off the holes so they didn't freeze back up. There was one touch of civilization in the wet carpeting on the floor.

I helped him carry the gear in. There was a car battery that had spent the night sucking juice from a charging unit in his basement, a TV, a CB, a sonar fish finder, a gas-operated auger, two electric light bulbs, a 25-pound LP gas tank with attached heater and three white five-gallon buckets. Mr. Z said that the kids in the area stole anything that was not nailed down, so he never left anything valuable in the house.

One bucket was filled with fishing gear and the other two were filled with beer. The beer buckets each had secondary functions once the beer was removed. If all went well, the first beer bucket would soon be filled with fish. Mr. Z explained that sometimes you didn't catch enough fish to take home, and if the fish were kept alive, they could still be released. I later found out that this was illegal, but I also discovered it to be a common practice among the ice fishers I visited.

The third bucket would be filled with minnows for bait.

Mr. Z put the auger to work as soon as we got there. There were four square openings in the plywood floor of the house, and Mr. Z lowered the auger through them one by one and drilled the fishing holes through the ice. He went outside and drilled another hole about twenty feet away. This was just in case we wanted to add a tip-up later in the day for some outside fishing.

Inside the house, the LP heater had set up a cycle of freeze-and-thaw. The place heated up like a sweat lodge until we turned the heater off, and then my wet knees would get cold and we'd turn it back on. Off and on all day long.

To keep his minnow supply at the house, Mr. Z had a plastic one-gallon pickle jar punched full of holes with a nylon rope tied through a hole in the lid. He bored a hole outside the house, put a rock in the jar for ballast, filled it with minnows, and then dropped the jar down into the water with the rope tied to a corner of the hut.

Before we started to fish, he reached down the corner hole with a coat hanger, snagged the minnow rope, and brought up the pickle jar. He then dumped a batch of minnows into the plastic bucket and we baited our hooks.

"Hey, Roger, this one has a hole through its back and it's still alive."

"Yeah, that's how you hook them. You put the hook through the minnow's back with the front of the hook toward the front of the minnow. Fish always swallow their meal head first." As I got farther along in my ice fishing research I found this was not the only way to present a minnow. At this point, however, I accepted Z's method as the last word in minnow hooking.

There were a couple of rough benches, and we sat facing each other while we fished. Mr. Z had let his line down the hole closest to the door. His fishing rig was definitely the no-frills, economy model. The line was still on the plastic spool the way it came from the store, the hook was plain, the sinker was small and the minnow was unadorned. A simple bobber kept the bait two feet off the bottom. There was no rod, no jigging stick, no rattle reel; just the plain plastic spool, hung on a nail on the wall.

I noticed that there was an 18-inch graphite rod with an expensive-looking Japanese casting reel inside the plastic bucket with the rest of the fishing gear. He said that it belonged to his son. Mr. Z never used it; he preferred to keep it simple and pull in his fish hand over hand the old-fashioned way.

While I was checking out the details of the house, I didn't notice that my bobber had gone down. Mr. Z had grabbed my line before I knew

I had a bite. "You got one!" he yelled as he yanked the fish out of the water. It was a crappie about eight inches long.

"I heard you do this to get away from your wife."

"Where did you hear that?"

"I don't remember," I lied.

Mr. Z explained that it was his first wife who he used to want to get away from. His present wife, Patty, liked to ice fish, as did some of their couple friends. Next year he planned to make the hut two-and-a-half times bigger. Maybe he would put a toilet in the corner. He said that the women didn't like peeing in the coffee can.

Two weeks later I ran into Mr. Z at a Holiday Gas Station. I told him I was going to Ely to see one of his former students at Vermillion College where the men in the dorm go ice fishing for trout every morning before classes. Mr. Z said that when he was in college in Bemidji they had to outlaw ice fishing for the students in his dorm. They didn't actually ban fishing, but they did forbid bringing fish into the dorm, because the place had started to stink. Every morning there had been a waiting line outside the utility room where the guys cleaned their fish.

He told me about the First Annual "Z" Ice Fishing Contest that was held a week earlier. Mr. Z and Patty and three other couples had been the only entrants. It was the women against the men, and each team was allowed to fish in the house for three hours. Patty ended up with a five-pound northern and the right to keep the trophy until next year's contest. The guys put up a board and played poker during their three-hour shift, but when they hooked their second-place, four-pound northern, no one wanted to leave the game to land it. Mr. Z said, "The wives beat the gents and they kept pouring salt in the wounds, but we stayed all night and it was a really good time."

"Space Between Red and Yellow," 72x72" - oil on canvas, by Dale Johnson

Another Fishouse Artist

Several museums will show an ice fishing art exhibition of Larry's silkscreened fishouse prints and the work of other artists. In his search for art for the show Larry found Dale Johnson, an ice fishing painter who teaches in St. Paul.

Dale asked me how long I had been working on this ice fishing business. I told him it had been about three years.

"Well, I've been working on the same thing for six years."

It turned out that he actually had been working longer than that, and he seemed to feel that I was invading his turf. Since artists are as territorial as wolves, it took a while for me to convince him that there was enough room on the ice for both of us.

As we talked he told me that he had been painting fishouses for a long time. He also had recently given a silkscreen course at the college where he taught. I told him that I had been a silkscreen artist for twenty-one years. He had recently started a series of silkscreen prints of fishouses. I told him I had done the same. He told me that my name kept coming up in conversations and I told him that his did too. We began to talk like old friends, and he invited me to his studio where he spoke to me about ice fishing.

"I look like an ice fisherman, but I'm really an artist who's disguised as a fisherman. I'm doing observations of this phenomenal subculture I've discovered. I've been working on it since '83 all through the winters and even into the summers. In order to paint I have had to cut a big window in the fishouse which is larger than the normal ones. I'm one of the only guys out there with a picture window. Everybody else has windows that are just big enough to check on the weather and keep an eye on their tip-ups. Mine is big because I'm out there painting the panoramics and the dialogue between the fishouses and the fishermen. So I want to look out that window. I have a way of closing it when people come, for a certain amount of privacy.

"One day I was peering out and painting and I had five small paintings started. Two of them were looking real good and I didn't want to be bothered. I heard this *whooump, whooump, whooump* coming around the shanty. I couldn't see who it was and I didn't want to talk to anyone, so I slipped this piece of Styrofoam into the window and I clicked the lock. You aren't supposed to have a lock, but I have one anyway. The game warden has talked to me about it several times, but so far I haven't taken it off. Anyway, what happened was he tapped on the door and said, 'How you doing? Any luck?' I couldn't think of what to say. I didn't want to talk to anyone, and I thought that if he saw what I was doing he'd announce it to everyone and he'd tell me about the uncle who couldn't draw a straight line and all those other stories, and I just didn't want to get into that. I looked around and saw the two small paintings I had set aside and said, 'I've got two small ones, but it's going pretty slow.' He expected me to come out and greet him more properly, but I didn't say anything and pretty soon I heard *whooump, whooump, whooump* and he was gone.

"Some people have heard about what I'm doing. They don't understand why I'm painting fishhouses, but I find them fascinating; there is a certain kind of simplicity. These are transient communities that move around with the fishing. The dialogue is all about catching fish, yet there is something else going on. There is a camaraderie here. People actually invite me into their place, or I invite them into mine and tell them some of the things that I've done to catch fish. They share with me their wonderful little truths, things which have taken years to perfect. They offer me conversation and a beer or coffee. Maybe we have a common problem of theft or other skullduggery such as trashing the shanties.

"I find ice fishing and painting confusing and wonderful and intriguing, because I'm not always clear which one I'm doing. I'm painting and I have a tip-up out, and when I'm looking out there I'm not sure if I'm looking to see if I'm catching something or observing the space between the shanties and the light and whatever else I need to be aware of to paint.

"I also paint what I see when I look down the hole. I cut a large square hole and I throw sand on the bottom of the lake through the hole. It gives me a light-colored ground on which to view the fish and that helps with both the fishing and the painting.

"My fishhouse is really a shanty, studio, study, and retreat. I have a large map of the stars on the ceiling. In the summertime, I keep my fishhouse next door to my house. Whenever I get mad at my wife or my kids, I go out there and lie on the floor and look at the stars. I never stay mad long."

"Afternoon Fishing," charcoal on paper, by Dale Johnson

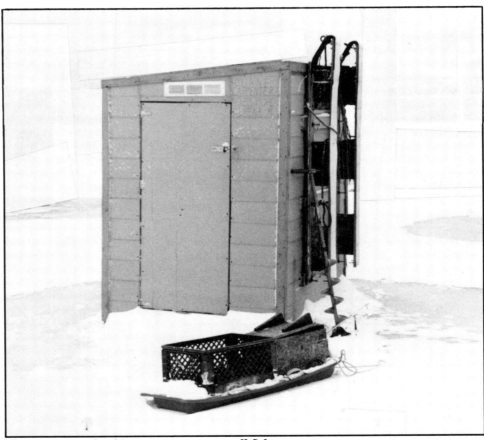

The runners make this an easy-on, easy-off fishhouse

The Poacher

To some people it is simply God's Country. To the state of Minnesota it is the Land of 10,000 Lakes. Actually there are 15,291 lakes in the state that are ten acres or larger. These include scores of lakes named Round, Bass, Big and Fish, and one hundred twenty-two named Rice.

God filled these lakes with millions of fish, and He also created thousands of fishermen to catch them. The state of Minnesota then created rule books and fishing licenses and game wardens. God, in turn, hoping to get the last word, created poachers.

This incident on one of Minnesota's Rice Lakes involved a poacher and five game wardens. Everyone's name has been changed to protect the authors.

Pete Aspen, a fisherman, a hunter, and often a poacher, loved to take more than his fair share of walleye out of Rice Lake, but he was careful not to get caught. However, Pete drank a lot and he talked a lot, so most of his secrets became known all over the county. Over the thirty-year period that he fished this lake, five different game wardens worked the territory. Each tried to nail Pete, but they could never catch him doing anything wrong. When one warden passed the mantle to the next man, he also passed on the folklore about Pete. As Pete got older, the game wardens got younger, but they never caught him doing any of the things he bragged about uptown.

Al, the fifth warden to work Rice Lake during Pete's fishing career, was not only new to the area, but a rookie warden. After days of collecting stories from the previous warden, he decided to be the one to bring Pete down.

The young warden planned to attack Pete on Rice Lake. He suspected that Pete might have left some fishing lines in the water overnight inside his fishhouse. In Minnesota you must be within eighty feet of any lines you have in the water. Usually, a game warden looking for illegal lines inside a fishhouse will drill a hole through the ice alongside the house and then take a bent wire like a giant coat hanger, and sweep it under the house to snag any lines in the water. Next he will sit in his car until the suspect arrives so he can write the summons.

Al was not going to mess around with drilling holes in the ice and sweeping the water with wires. Even though it was illegal for game wardens at the time, he had a master set of keys to unlock any door. He opened Pete's fishhouse and, just as he suspected, there was a line left in the water. He closed the door and waited. It seemed forever, because he was so excited being a young warden on the verge of writing a ticket for this legendary poacher.

When Pete showed up, Al was there to issue the summons. Pete was furious. While Al was writing it up, Pete walked around the fishouse searching for the standard game warden line-checking hole, which he did not find. Al told him to sign the summons. Pete refused, "You entered my house illegally."

"You left a line in the water untended."

Al threatened him with everything in his rookie game warden repertoire. Pete knew his rights and he stood firm. Al went back to his game warden car and got his game warden billy club and waved it under Pete's nose. Pete still refused to sign the ticket. The warden went to the car for his game warden pistol, and he waved it just as he had waved his billy club, but Pete stood firm.

It was a fishouse standoff, but Pete was required to go to court. Al was there in his game warden suit and tie and the two of them squared off again. Pete claimed that his own brother's son had left the line in the water, and his brother was there to agree. Then Pete said that he thought his lock had been picked because there was no sign of a game warden hole outside his house. He also told the judge about the game warden gun that Al had been waving around at the end of the encounter. Pete said he was prepared to bring Al back to this same court for trespassing and brandishing a pistol in a careless manner.

Al was taken by surprise. He expected to be a hero for catching Pete, but now he was accused of trespassing. Reluctantly, he admitted to breaking and entering. The judge was disappointed. He knew that Pete was a famous poacher, but he also knew the law. "Case dismissed," he said, glowering at Al.

Mining the Lake

JJ Johnson is a teacher in a small town near the Canadian border. His fishing buddies all call him Crazy JJ, and he thinks of himself as a fishing outlaw. In this story JJ explains some of the tricks of the poaching trade and tells how he first met Pete Aspen. We changed the names in this one to stay out of trouble with the Minnesota Walleye Mafia.

I was ice fishing in Canada with Axel, the principal of the school where I teach. We went up on a Friday afternoon to Lost Lake and put in a couple of lines near the island. You've probably never seen anything like the set-ups we use. They're a lot different than a tip-up, and we call them mousetraps. We made them out of brazed rod, and they looked like flat thread-bobbins. I was only twenty years old when I learned how to make them from an old warden who is long dead.

I taught a shop class at the school and I told the kids we were making these hanging, brazed metal photo frames for their projects. At the end of the semester I told them there had been a change in plans and they wouldn't be able to take their projects home. And that's how we built up our mousetrap inventory.

On the Canadian trip we set up two mousetraps on Friday night and hid them so they couldn't be seen. Saturday morning the lines were still untouched, so we re-hid them and went to another lake and fished all day. When we came back in the afternoon, there were two guys we had never seen before standing by the island fishing.

It's no secret that I used to be an outlaw, but now I've gone straight. I've even worked with the game wardens and shown them some of my tricks. You know, some of the best game wardens are actually reformed outlaws.

Anyway, this is how we set up those mousetraps. We would take our snow machines out on the lake, one following the other, so that there was only one track. Axel would go first and I would stop my machine so there was only a short distance between the two of us. I put one foot on the back bumper of Axel's machine and the other foot on the front bumper of mine, never putting a footprint in the snow, while I augured a hole through the ice.

Then I would take a 12x12-inch piece of white quarter-inch paneling, tie the mousetrap to it, put it over the hole with the white side up and cover it with snow. I drove my snow machine over it until there wasn't any evidence that we had stopped there. We then went three snowmobile-lengths past the set-up and made a mark in the snow or we would take a chunk of ice and throw it off to one side. Sometimes when a storm came up, we would have to spend forty-five minutes to an hour looking for the holes, but in all the years of fishing we never lost a set-up.

Anyway, when we came back to the island where the set-ups were, there were these two strangers standing there fishing. Not knowing what to do, we decided to go over and talk to them. After a couple of minutes of small talk, the bigger of the two guys asked me if I was Crazy JJ. I said that some people had called me that, but I wondered how he had heard of me since I had never seen him before on this lake. The big guy said that it was his first trip to this part of the country and that he had stopped at the lodge/resort/general-store/bait-shop where Bob, the owner, had told him that if he wanted to fish lake trout, he had to talk to Crazy JJ. I was madder than hell at Bob for opening his mouth, but after we talked for a while I realized we had some things in common. The big guy introduced himself as Pete Aspen and said the old guy with him was Maury. I asked Pete if he had any fish.

"You know something? We have twenty-one lines out here right now. We've mined this lake."

I asked Pete what kind of rig he was using, and he described an old version of the mousetrap that I had heard of but never tried. Pete took coffee cans and wrapped the line around them. The fish would take the bait and pull the line out from under the rubber band that was holding it in place. Pete and Maury said they'd been fishing since early that morning with that rig. They had a tent set up, and they were going to fish all week on Lost Lake. Pete said, "We haven't got a fish."

"Sometimes it works that way. I'll tell you what, we got two lines sitting here, and we've got to pull them up."

Pete asked where they were and I said, "You're standing on one of them." Well, Pete thought I was putting him on, but he moved anyway. I reached down, scraped the snow from the board, pulled it up, and sure enough the line was all stripped off the mousetrap. It took about fifteen minutes to land the fish. Pete just stood there saying over and over, "I don't believe this, I don't believe this. It's not happening."

I pulled in the lake trout, a seventeen-pounder.

Pete said, "I got to get a picture of that."

"We've got another line about two hundred yards over there."

Axel went over to that one, uncovered it and hollered back, "Hey, this one is all stripped out, too." By the time we all got over there, Axel had the line halfway in. He said, "JJ, this looks like another pretty good fish."

He pulled up a fifteen-pounder, and Pete said, "If I didn't see it, I wouldn't believe it."

Pete wanted to know what he was doing wrong. There wasn't a thing on any of his twenty-one lines. It turned out that he was using smelt for bait. I told him that the trout in Lost Lake wouldn't touch smelt because they weren't native; these trout didn't know what smelt were. Axel and I always used cisco, a freshwater herring common to all the lakes in the area.

Pete took a picture of Axel and me with our fish, and a few weeks later he sent us a copy. So that's how I first met Pete and that's when he started using our kind of mousetrap and cisco for bait.

Before I went straight, Pete and I got together at least once a year to compare notes and mine another lake. They ran Pete out of here several years ago, but there are still a couple of places where they don't know who he is.

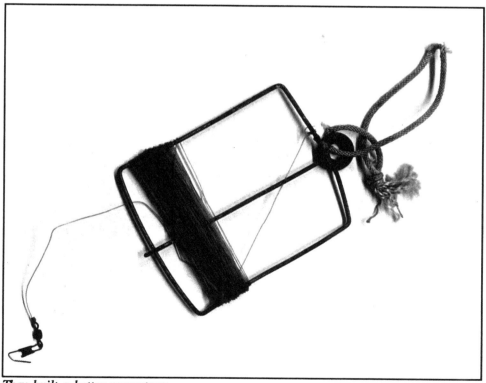

They built a better mousetrap

Any "port" in a storm?

Crazy JJ Goes Straight

It's the end of an era, and Crazy JJ Johnson is caught between the new technology and an old game warden with a new attitude.

Axel and I had gone up into Canada late in the winter. The snow was gone on most of the portages, but the ice was still okay. We took our snow machines, and we had a devil of a time getting over the portages. It was mostly rocks and no snow, and it really tore up the machines.

When we got to the lake, I said to Axel, "We got nothing to worry about, there aren't going to be any game wardens around this weekend, not a thing to worry about." So we put a couple of lines out and we didn't cover them or anything. I admit it, we got careless and lazy.

This was a Saturday, and we left about ten lines in the lake. We didn't use any of our mousetrap covers, just left them all out there in the open. Sunday morning two of our friends went up about 6:30 to the narrows. They hadn't been fishing very long when the Canadian game warden came along. He just appeared out of nowhere and said he wanted to check them out. He had been out on the lake late Saturday afternoon, found the lines we left out, and now he was looking for poachers. Our friends played dumb, and since they weren't doing anything wrong, he left them and headed out onto the lake.

About the same time, Axel and I came tooling up to the lake on our machines, and as soon as we got to the first hole I could see that something was wrong. It had been a cold night and there should have been a layer of fresh ice covering the hole. It was obvious that the ice had recently been broken. Since I had already decided that there wasn't any way the game warden would have come this far, I figured that the other guys had checked our lines before going up to the narrows to fish.

I left the line in the water and we got the auger to put in a couple more lines. Axel looked up and saw a little black spot on the horizon. Sure enough there was a snow machine coming over the lake. Pretty soon it got close enough for us to recognize the driver. It was Jamie, the game warden. It was too late in the season for him to be out, but there he was sitting right in front of us.

"Hi, JJ. I figured it was you."

I told him that I would have bet good money that he wouldn't be showing up this late in the season, especially on a Sunday. He just smiled, and we made small talk for a while before he wandered out to where the fishing holes were. Well, when I had first seen him coming, I'd had enough sense to grab the lines and stash them in the engine compartment of my machine right next to the muffler. Anyway he walked out to the hole and there was no tip-up, no rod, and no fishing line. He went to the other hole and saw that it was empty too.

Jamie came back and said, "JJ, where are the lines that were in those holes?"

"Jamie, I don't know what holes you're talking about, we just got here."

"JJ, look at those footprints going out to the hole. Those bootprints are just exactly like what you've got on."

"Jamie! These are Sorels; every fisherman who comes up here wears Sorels. There's no way those are my footprints. Those were made by someone else." Jamie and I were both getting a little embarrassed, because we have known each other for a long time, and we consider ourselves friends even though Jamie is a warden.

Jamie said, "Those are your footprints."

I knew he didn't have a case against us. He walked around kicking snow and looking for the set-ups. He checked the snow machines. We all knew he had a legal right to check the packs and everything, and he did just that, but somehow he never thought to lift the hood.

We felt foolish. How could we explain the fact that we were out here in the middle of the wilderness sitting on the bank of a frozen lake watching a couple of empty fish holes? And how did we explain that we didn't have any tip-ups or lines in our packs? Jamie knew that we were up to no good, but he had to catch us in the act if he was going to write us up. He finally said to me, "JJ, we've been friends for a long time, but I gotta give you a ticket."

"But you don't have any grounds to give me a ticket."

"Those are your bootprints going out there."

"As far as I'm concerned, you don't have any evidence," I said. Axel and I just sat there while he wrote the ticket. I was feeling kind of bad too, because, after all, I was guilty as hell. Jamie asked me to sign the ticket, and I refused. "I'm not signing anything." Jamie told me that if I signed it I was just acknowledging the fact that the ticket was issued, but I still wouldn't sign it. Jamie gave me the ticket and told me where I would have to go to court. I was lying through my teeth, but I still said, "Jamie, I'm not guilty."

Before we went back to the states, I talked to some other Canadian wardens who told me that there wasn't any way Jamie could have arrested me. But I still got a letter from the court about two months later saying that I had been found guilty and I was to pay thirty-five dollars. I just threw it away. I wasn't going to go clear back up there to court for a lousy thirty-five-dollar fine. About three months after that, I got another letter, this time from a court closer to where I live, stating that I had a second chance to come and defend myself. They were actually pretty nice. They went to a lot of trouble to explain the court system and how I would be able to go one-on-one with the judge. There wasn't a chance I would lose. I started to worry. Hunting season was coming on; I hunt in Canada, and I wouldn't be able to go back there if I didn't go to court or pay the fine.

I put it off as long as I could, waiting to send my check until early in the fall. Jamie knew that I went duck hunting in his area, and I figured that he would be looking for me. So finally, a week before hunting season started, I sent the money along with a letter that stated that I was not guilty. After the deduction for the exchange rate, it cost me twenty-six bucks. I even got a thank you letter from them.

A week later, Axel and I were sitting in our boat there on the river hunting, and sure enough, up the river comes Jamie in his boat. He looked really nervous.

"Hi, JJ. How are things going?" He scratched his head and just sat there looking at us. Finally, he said, "JJ, there's a warrant for your arrest on the dash of my truck."

I said, "Jamie, I'll put your mind at ease. I paid it a week ago."

"Geeze, did you really pay it?"

"Yes. You don't have to worry anymore."

After that, the wardens changed their tactics. They couldn't pin anything on us, but someone must have been tipping them off because they really started to turn up the heat. Once, I was fishing with some friends at a nice spot where there was a high wall to keep the wind down, and we built a fire because it was so cold. We wanted to stay on shore by the fire. The lines were out and I knew they were over two hundred feet away, which is illegal in Canada. I looked down the lake and I saw this machine coming. I quick got on my machine and went out there. They saw me and sure enough it was Jamie, and he was riding with the American warden. I don't know why they were together, but sometimes they rode together on the border lakes. That way if someone said, "I'm on the American side," they could say, "Okay, he's the American warden."

Anyhow, we talked for a while and Jamie said, "JJ, show me the insurance papers for your machine." Canada had passed a law the year before that you could not go into Canada without liability insurance. I knew that, but thought it shouldn't matter in an area as sparsely populated as that was, so I didn't have insurance.

I said, "Jamie! What are you talking about?"

"JJ, it's the law, you gotta have insurance in Canada. It's a $105 fine if you don't have it."

"Jamie! I don't have insurance. I never knew you had to have it."

He looked at me and said, "I think you did know about it, but I'm not going to do anything about it this time. Tell me where your helmet is."

I didn't have my helmet on. It wasn't even on my machine. I said, "It's back at the fire." There is a law in Canada that whenever you get on your snowmobile and go any place, you have to have your helmet on.

I knew what he was doing, and I knew he had seen me drive out to the holes; in fact, what he was doing was telling me to shape up. I looked at the American warden who was also a friend, and he just shrugged his shoulders as if to say it wasn't his problem, and I said to Jamie, "Okay. Fine. From now on you can have the lake. I'm done. Canada is getting too picky for me." And that was the last time I was trout fishing up there. Let's face it, it just wasn't fun anymore...

The bare minimum

Two-for-One Trout

JJ had a knack for hooking lake trout. Even when he wasn't poaching he seemed to get more than his fair share. In this story he reveals some unorthodox methods for doubling his catch.

My friend Axel and I were out on Round Lake, and I caught two trout on one line. At first I couldn't figure out how it happened. I had one line out with only one hook. We watched the line spin off the reel and we stood there and waited until it stopped. It seemed like it took a good four or five minutes. When I started to pull it in, it came in fairly easy, but all of a sudden it got heavier, and I said, "Axel, this is a lot bigger than I thought."

I pulled in the rest of the line, and up through the hole came a six-pound trout. But when I got it on the ice there was more fishing line in the hole, and I wondered what was going on. It looked like it was coming out of the trout's mouth and going right back into the water. I picked up this extra line and started working it in, and it felt like I had another fish. There was at least thirty feet of line out, and it took a while to get it all in. Finally I got to the end and out comes another six-pound trout.

Axel said, "How in the hell did you do that?"

We went back and looked more closely at the first six-pounder. The fishing line had made a half hitch around its gill; it wasn't hooked anywhere. We figured that even though it came up the hole first, it had actually been caught second. Somehow, while the trout we caught on the hook was circling around, it tied a knot around that fish's gill. It makes sense. I've fished in a darkhouse and I've watched what happens when I've snagged a big one. If there are other fish there, they just swim close by and watch it try to shake loose. Maybe the trout that got caught in the line had just hung around too long.

Another time I was up fishing with my friend Oscar who had these expensive reels and fancy short rods. We were eating and not paying attention to the holes when a trout hit the bait and took it all the way to the end of the line and then yanked Oscar's rod and reel down through the hole and into the water. Oscar was crying about his $30 reel and his graphite rod, but there was nothing we could do about it.

I happen to know that when a trout pulls a rod down a hole, the rod and reel go to the bottom and the weight of the outfit keeps the fish in the same area. Depending on how much line is out, they will have a radius of fifty or sixty yards in which to swim around. The rod and reel will move around some, but not much. Even if they move a little, the trout will go first one way and then another, so the general area where the equipment is doesn't change much.

A week later, Axel and I went up and we fished the same spot where Oscar lost his stuff. I caught a fish and I'm not sure what happened next, whether the fish swam around the line or if the fish that stole Oscar's rod and reel swam around my line, but somehow the lines got tangled up and when I brought my fish out of the hole I found this other line wrapped around it. When I brought the other line in, there was a trout on one end and Oscar's rod and reel on the other. On the way home, I stopped and gave Oscar his outfit. He couldn't believe it. I thought that there might be some question about who owned the trout that was hooked to the rod and reel, but I didn't mention it and Oscar was so excited about getting his gear back that he forgot to ask.

All this and TV, too

The Iceman

"I've seen guys sitting in their fish shacks when the ice cracks and their cars fall right in. Oh, yeah that's the truth. It's an experience." Hank the Iceman is talking. He's got his arms folded across his chest and a wad of chew under his lower lip. Hank and his wife Linda own the Lakeside resort on Minnesota's Mille Lacs Lake. "I've seen seven cars fall in all in one day, all within five minutes...it's not a game out there. In 1982 there was fifty-two cars went in the lake. Three people drowned."

Hank is standing behind the bar at his resort. It's the middle of the summer and Hank's son is cutting a hole through the floor behind the bar taking out some rot and patching things up. Hank tells him to turn off the reciprocating saw so he can hear. Linda takes a video they shot over the winter of '88/'89, puts it into the VCR and rotates the big screen TV so it is showing behind Hank as he talks about the ice.

On the screen Hank has a tall, red knit cap and a black Mennonite beard. There is footage showing his remodeled, ten-geared, six-wheel-drive geologic survey truck that he got for $1900. He is plowing the ice and towing people's fishhouses out onto the lake. The houses are built on wooden runners like giant sleds. On the video the plow is hung up on a bank of snow turned to ice, so jammed up in the hard snow Hank can't budge it. The voice on the video is saying, "It's just another day in the life of a guy on the snow."

The resort is open winter and summer, but it doesn't take long to figure that Hank is happier in the winter. He's a good pilot in the summer at the helm of one of his fishing launches, but he is legendary on the ice with his converted geologic survey truck with its brakes all frozen up, ground blizzards swirling and pressure ridges popping and booming across the lake.

When the lake is beginning to freeze, the changing winds break the ice open, leaving ice-free areas of water. When the ice comes back together, it is with such force that the ice pushes up over itself and forms long ridges that run off into the distance. These are the pressure ridges that the icemen talk about. Sometimes they are just bumps or humps, and sometimes they are six- to eight-inch thick vertical pieces of ice sticking up off the lake and through the snow. At times, the sun shines through these ice protrusions making them sparkle like giant diamonds or pieces of fractured crystal.

"There's cracks out there where the ice expands and contracts," Hank says. "It happens every day. They've lost cars in this lake through cracks in twenty-four inches of ice."

Hank points to the picture of snow and ice on the video. "Don't let that little two-inch crack fool you; that devil's about four-foot wide there. It expanded and contracted all winter, that bugger. One night after we packed it with snow I had a guy pulling out his own shack. I told him, 'You follow me. Don't go out without me. If I make a sharp turn suddenly then you follow me.'"

Hank shook his head as if he couldn't believe how ignorant some people can be. "You don't get to be an iceman overnight. You gotta know what you're doing. You can't take your eyes off the ice - you see a little hairline crack start to develop, you got to move right now.

"Well, the first thing I know, this guy has taken off without me. He got out about a hundred feet onto the ice, and a crack started under his car and he went right in. The motor was still running under the water, the fan was churning away until the carburetor went under." With his hands, Hank made a picture of the ice opening up and the car sliding in. "They fall slow, so you usually have time to get out.

"You wait till there is ten inches of ice before you drive on the lake. When the ice is thick enough and it cracks, the piece you are on catches on the bottom of the other piece and it binds. If the ice is too thin it slips right by. When the ice binds, that's when you decide whether to jump or ride it out. It's like playing Russian roulette out there. I'm not joking."

Hank has fallen all the way through the ice only once, and he is reluctant to talk about it. He says, "Most of the time when the ice breaks under you, you stick with the truck. If you're lucky you get out. If you're not, you go down. I've only been down once; the rest of the times I've made it out.

"One time I was towing a house when the ice broke. The water in the cab was up to the seat. There had to be fifty, sixty feet of broken ice, and I just kept the front wheels reaching for the solid edge. I kept grabbing at it. The ice drops slow, you know, and I was ready to jump out, but the front wheels finally grabbed hold and pulled me out. It's an experience, let me tell you, it's an experience."

Hank spit into the garbage can behind the bar for emphasis. On the video his son is towing a house onto the ice. The road they have plowed looks like a landing strip.

Hank sounds more and more like the kind of guy you want to have around when you get in a jam. He smiles and tells the story of pulling a flier out of the drink in Vietnam. There were thirty-foot seas and his commander had told him to turn back. "There was no way I was going back," said Hank. "I knew I could get him." In his nearly twenty years on Mille Lacs he has saved seven people. "Last June I found three kids and a guy out there in the water. They were blue, but they made it."

On the video the Iceman is augering a hole in one of the rental units. The auger has a twenty-four-volt motor from a World War II bomber on it. Only the Iceman can handle it. Anyone else would be whipped around the hole.

"Once I was cleaning a hole for the highway patrol guy who had rented the cabin and I didn't realize that someone had left a line in the water, and when I hit reverse, the line wrapped around the auger. I felt this tugging and when I looked down the hole there was a walleye hanging there. I told the highway patrol 'hurry up, they're jumping out of the hole!' The highway patrol looked in the cabin and said, 'My God, they are!' That was the only fish he got the whole trip."

Hank says that this resort was one of the first to have fishhouses. "Windy Johnson used to haul guys out with his sleigh. He'd haul them out in the morning and bring them back at night. Now there are people who stay out there all winter. We keep track of them here with this rack of cards. If the card is turned backward you can see it from anywhere in the room, and we know they're out on the ice. Someone calls up and we can tell if the person they're looking for is here. Sometimes we are out there on the ice and we can't move the trucks, and we have to leave them there. At the same time the people can't get in here to the dining room, but they do okay. They've got microwaves, bars, little pumps for their running water. A bunch of them will go together and share a generator. Sometimes we even bring dinners out to them when they're stuck on the ice, prime rib and potatoes. Or a storm will come up and we will have a bunch of folks stuck in **here**, forty or fifty of them sleeping on the floor. We keep the bar open all night."

The Iceman talks about making music at New Year's when it is thirty below. He says the resort's volunteer band makes pretty good music. A shot of his "stomp fiddle" on the screen looks like a cross between a washtub bass and a coat rack.

"By New Year's the ice is pretty thick, but it still will break. When we plow the roads we pile the snow on the south side until the weight breaks the ice. The snow sinks the ice and then the road rises and we get a crown. The only problem is that if you get too close to the edge crack, your front wheel will fall in. I've never lost a vehicle while road plowing," he says, "but I've had them in over the headlights."

Hank says that when you let your truck sit for a while in one spot on the ice, you actually make a big dimple as the ice bends and flexes. Several vehicles standing together make a bigger dimple. "When you're driving out there you can watch the truck ahead of you drop down. There's a lot of flexibility to the ice. You got to separate the cars and keep them apart. The ice gets to slapping and builds up a rhythm of its own."

On the screen the camera pans across the snow-covered ice. There is not a car or a fishhouse in sight. Linda looks at the screen and says, "Sometimes it is like working on the tundra."

Hank says, "We don't allow anybody to move their own shacks once they're out there. We got to know where everybody is, and we want all the doors to face southeast. That way if you get lost in a blizzard you can always tell where you are when you come up to someone's house. A compass does not always work out there on the lake. When you're lost out there and the snow is swirling around the truck, you can't even tell the direction of the wind. The iceman who taught me had twenty-seven years on the ice. He would take a roll of toilet paper and get away from the truck and unroll it to see the wind direction, and then he'd radio back to the resort and they'd tell him which direction the wind was blowing and he could find his way back. We've used the same trick to get back in the launch in the summertime. The lake is on a plateau, and the clouds often come right down to the water. You can't see a thing. The compass spins in circles. It's something to do with the static electricity. Your monofilament line will go straight up in the air like a kite string. A graphite rod will snap a spark four inches from your hand. You've got to keep the pole in the water to keep it grounded." Hank put his finger up in the air like a graphite fishing pole.

On the video it was February already, and they were plowing the snow away from the fishhouses getting ready to drag them off the ice. The guys hooking up the towing cables to the houses were working on water-covered ice.

Hank pointed to himself on the video and said, "It's hard to keep your feet warm out there. We got over fifty miles of plowed roads, and sometimes we have been out there for thirty-six hours straight. There's only one kind of boot to use. The water can be standing two feet deep on top of the ice. So we use those Air Force bunny boots, the inflatable ones. That's all you can wear out there. We don't put air in them, but when you're sloshing around in the water all day, they're the only thing that keep your feet from freezing.

"One year when we took the houses off, there were white caps on the water over the ice. It's no joke to be driving on the ice when the water is so deep that the mattresses are floating out the fishhouse doors. Now that's an eerie feeling."

Hank grins and says, "You wouldn't believe it unless you've seen it. It's an experience. You bet."

A treacherously beautiful pressure ridge on Mille Lacs Lake

DE LUXE FISH HOUSE IS AGAIN ON THE LAKE

Bill Lipetzky and Joe Lindholm have their de luxe fish house out on the Lake. Many improvements have been installed for this season, including a new heating plant and kitchenette. There is so much snow that it was hard to get the thing on the Lake, and the boys almost decided to set it up on a vacant lot, where it would be easier to visit. The only reason for having it on the Lake is that the water supply is more convenient, and it is not believed that this is very important. They admit they never get any fish, but claim they like the fresh air and fine view from the Lake.

The Isle Advance
Mille Lacs Lake at
Isle, Minnesota
Thursday, Dec. 22, 1927

Eelpout and Garlic Butter

Wintertime patrons at the Agate Bay Resort on Minnesota's Mille Lacs Lake call them "the girls." Their real names are Penny and Lori, and they come up every weekend during ice fishing season and live in their 10x16-foot fishhouse. It's an attractive place with ivory aluminum siding, brown trim, a white storm door and a TV antenna on the roof. Lori, who has been fishing for twenty-eight years, says that it has everything but a man and running water. The fishhouse was part of her divorce settlement. She told her husband that he could have everything they owned except the fishing boat and the fishhouse and she would cut him up in little pieces and put him in sandwich bags if she didn't get the fishhouse.

Lori and Penny have the knack for catching walleye. They say there is no secret to it; they simply catch fish when no one else does. Penny, who has now been fishing for four years with Lori, says it's hard on some of the men. The old timers say, "The girls have fish. Talk to the girls. They'll tell you how to do it."

It's also no secret that some people at the resort do not put their fishhouses out until Lori's is in place. Then they get as close as they can without being too obvious about it. Lori says, "Some of these people move their houses every week, looking for a better fishing spot, but we leave ours in the same place all winter. Every now and then there is a knock on the door and some poor soul says, 'Can I just sit here and watch for awhile?' Or someone else will say, 'Can I take a look? I've never seen a walleye before.' Sometimes I feel so sorry for them that I let them pull in the fish for me. We catch a lot of fish!"

Minnesotans love walleye. They drive hundreds of miles in the wee hours and eat bad muffins at gas station food marts. They put hooks through live minnows and freeze their butts off on the ice just to catch a fair-sized, bug-eyed fish from the perch family.

People here like to eat them fresh, though they still taste good after being frozen. Nowadays you can't just clean your walleye and cook it up. You have to take it off the ice to clean it. There is a 20-inch rule on Mille Lacs which allows one fish over twenty inches per person per day. If you clean them and eat them, the game warden can't tell if you're breaking the 20-inch rule. Since walleye taste better fresh, there is a certain amount of illegal eating going on at any given time. Lori and Penny catch their walleye and toss them out the door into the snow to freeze for the trip to shore.

To satisfy their craving for good fresh fish the women endorse eelpout as the catch of the day. A surprising number of people have never heard of eelpout, some people hate them, and a significant number of fishermen don't want to get close enough to decide whether they hate them or not. They pull the fish in just close enough to see its ugly face and then cut the line and let it loose. Lori wouldn't think of letting one go. She plops her bait on the bottom and prays. When she gets an eelpout, she drags it through the hole, throws it out the door, cuts her line and lets it freeze for about fifteen minutes. "If you don't do that," she says, "they wrap around your arm and coat you with slime. I can't deal with them when they're alive."

Call it burbot, lawyer or eelpout, but this freshwater cod is still a slimy, ugly, revulsive creature.

Lori fillets her eelpout, cuts it into chunks and throws it in boiling water for five minutes. She then broils the fish with garlic butter for thirty seconds. "You would think you're really eating something exotic," she says. "In fact, they call it poor man's lobster."

The women have a drink, play cribbage, nibble on the eelpout, and watch the TV news. Actually the TV is on all day long no matter what they are doing. Penny says that they never just sit and watch it, it's just on. Lori says it keeps them in tune with reality. The women are experts on reality, or rather how to get away from it. Realities, such as demanding husbands and kids with runny noses and long lines at the super market, are far-removed from the fishhouse. Lori and Penny sleep like babies with their fish lines dropping down through eighteen feet of freezing lake water. They wake up to pull in another walleye; they turn on the TV; they talk about their priorities. It may not be everyone's cup of tea, but for "the girls" it is a little bit of heaven.

Lori's Place, where the neighbors come to see the walleyes

The Ice Palace

Better-Than-Sex Cake

Larry's first visit to the ice fishing houses on Mille Lacs was in the winter of '88/'89. It's another one of those "I-had-a-friend-who-had-a-friend..." stories. Larry's friend Gene in Iowa had a friend who bought a house from a real estate agent who had a friend who owned half-interest in a fishouse on Mille Lacs Lake. So... Larry met Gary and Jimmy, co-owners of a class-act fishouse on Mille Lacs in central Minnesota.

There are resorts all around this 132,000-acre lake, each with its own ice fishing community to care for. They rent out fishouses, move and manage the privately-owned structures of their patrons and plow roads on the ice to keep the lifelines open for bread and beer. Over the winter thousands of fishouses spring up on the ice, and multi-laned roads run out in all directions.

I waited for my hosts at the Lakeside Resort, where I could see three or four hundred fishouses out on the lake through the picture windows. Gary, Jimmy and their friend Mac asked me to ride out with them to the fishouse. Hank, the owner of the resort, was asked to keep an eye on us and to come out with the snow plow if we got stuck. As it turned out, we got bogged down in some massive drifts a couple hundred feet away from the fishouse. They talked about "the cabin" while we waited for the plow.

I turned on the recorder and Jimmy launched into a stick-by-stick description of the construction of the fishouse. He said the 10x16-foot cabin was framed just like a house but on a smaller scale, with joists and rafters and a scissor-truss system for the roof.

While Jimmy was talking, I got lost in a snowy reverie. The billowing snow outside made it look like an Arctic ice field. The fishouses, the road and the ice all had disappeared from view. I wondered if you could get snow blindness sitting in a car. I worried about the car sitting for so long on the ice with the four of us in it and I tried to compute our weights and the weight of the car. The snow kept blowing, and there was no sign of the plow. How would Hank even find us? The wind chill factor had dropped to sixty below and suddenly I realized I wanted to get off the ice and go back to shore. Jimmy was discussing trusses when he apparently noticed the loss of my attention. He paused and said, "Look over there, it's the big place with the eight-in-twelve pitch roof." I looked and the fishouse was now visible in the sunlight. The whiteout was over.

Gary said that a nice thing about their house was the picture windows, two of which were Pella crank-outs designed for cross-ventilation in the summer. "On a day like today, you can sit inside in your T-shirt and look at the lake. It's entertainment, watching people out on the ice struggling, getting their cars stuck.

"At the end of the ice season, Hank will drag your fishouse right up on shore next to your favorite beach, and there you are, a fishouse on skids for winter and a cabin on the shoreline for summer."

Gary got so enthusiastic that he continued as narrator. "We were gonna put a bathroom in, but we figured we would have a lot of visitors coming over. So we still use the Port-a-Potty."

Hank finally arrived, plowing right by us creating a fishouse driveway. We followed him, piled out of the car and into the fishouse. Jimmy brought in a bakery box and set it on the counter. "What's that?" I asked.

"It's Better-Than-Sex Cake," said Gary.

"It's a tradition," said Jimmy.

The fishouse was as nice as they said it would be. Inside, I noticed holes for fishing; somehow this surprised me. With all the talk about the house and how well it was built, we hadn't even talked about fishing. Gary said, "The key thing up here is not so much catching fish. Actually, catching fish is just an extra. I can come here and not catch a fish and still have a hell of a good time. It's the getting away and talking and eating cake."

Once the holes were drilled out there were other chores to do. Mac scooped out the chopped ice that the auger had churned up and Jimmy started the 1000-watt Honda generator which sat outside the fishouse. The generator ran the lights, stereo unit, TV, outside lights and a battery charger, which was stored under the bed and used to charge a twelve-volt battery. At night they turned the generator off so they wouldn't have to get up every couple hours to gas it. They replaced all the AC light bulbs with DC bulbs run off the battery so if they got a nighttime fish they could land it without falling all over each other.

Next, we set the depth on the four fishing lines. There is no better way to get a heated discussion going among fishermen than to discuss the best way to do something, like how deep to set the lines. Every fisherman has a bag of theories that he keeps with his collection of fish stories along with a good supply of anecdotes to prove he's right. Mac said that the last person who used the house had been "killing" fish with his bait right on the bottom. Gary said his friend in Mankato fishes for walleye in forty feet of water with the bait twenty feet from the bottom. We proceeded to set the lines so the minnows would be about two feet from the bottom. This battle of the experts went on to how to hook a minnow.

Mac hooked his minnow up through the butt. "Owww!" we hollered in unison. "I'll bet that hurts!" His "bunghole" method really turned everyone off. That made three right ways of hooking a minnow I had learned since starting the book.

Mac was looking out the window as he fished. "This lake is pretty amazing. There are days when it is sunny out, but you can't see the shore because of the ground blizzard. It's real neat, but a little scary too. Years ago we used candles to light the holes and warm the air around them so the water wouldn't re-freeze. One evening, when I was staying up here in the old house, I had to go get some candles. There wasn't enough snow on the ice to define the roads, so I kept getting stuck and pushing myself out again. Finally, I got to the store and bought the candles. I started back towards the shanty, got lost and had to go back to shore. I got lost a second time and a third, and it was one o'clock in the morning by the time I found the place. Later on I was telling this story to Gary and Jimmy, and I found out they had a box of over a hundred candles under the bed. Now we have electrical outlets next to every hole to plug in the warming lights."

Jimmy points to the outlets and says, "Mr. High Tech. Yep! Mr. Gary High Tech."

Jimmy reminded us that we had been fishing for over two hours and only one little perch had been caught.

"It's mighty slow," said Gary.

Just then the bell rang, the jingle jingled, the rattle rattled. "There you go!" "Oh my!" "Wow! That's a nice perch." "That's a keeper."

They were wild men until the fish was put in a bucket of ice and the hook was re-baited. I looked in the perch's mouth and said, "Hey guys! This was caught on a minnow hooked the 'bunghole' way." For Mac it turned out to be a point to be proud of; by the end of the day all the lines were baited with the hook through the butt.

The camaraderie and competition between these three friends was interesting to watch. They said they took turns "answering the bell," but I noticed that they had all raced for the same line when that perch hit.

Gary confirmed that taking turns did not always work. "One night the bell went off and it was Jimmy's turn. He went for it, set the hook and said, 'This is a nice fish.' After he lost it he said, 'That was a nice fish. That thing was really heavy.'"

"Five minutes later, the bell went off again. Jimmy said, 'I'll get it.' I said, 'No! No! No! It's my turn.' I set the hook and thought, 'This is a nice fish.' After some fighting it was in, a seven-pounder. So Jimmy said in a crybaby voice, 'That should have been my fish.'"

Gary was just getting warmed up. "A couple of years ago in the

Boundary Waters, late at night during opening weekend, Jimmy caught a nice walleye. The next morning we went to weigh it and found it was nine pounds and some-odd ounces, a new record between us. A week later I caught one just as nice. He almost refused to get the net for me."

"Bullshit!"

"Anyway, to make a long story short, my fish weighed one ounce more than his."

"Yeah, but the woman who weighed it had a block of wood under the fish. We took the block of wood out and the fish weighed one ounce less."

"That's what Jimmy wants to believe, but it's not true. I had the woman sign a letter verifying the weight and I have twenty-five copies of this letter at home, hidden all over the house."

Mac said there was such a letter. He had seen a copy at Gary's place.

Jimmy said, "I saw that block of wood. I don't care if you have a hundred letters."

Gary said, "You can contact the BWCA canoe outfitters and they will tell you."

"Yeah! What does that prove? They probably have a copy of the same letter."

The "my-fish-was-bigger-than-your-fish" story went on until Jimmy related that his friend held a world record for catching the biggest fish, even though it was the ugliest. He was fishing on Lake of the Woods, reeled in a fish, took one look at it and disgustedly tried to kick it back down the hole. As he tried to get rid of the thing, a game warden walked up to him, looked at the fish and said, "That's a big eelpout. You ought to have it weighed." They took it to the local grocery store and sure enough, it was one-half ounce bigger than the previous world's record.

Gary said that in honor of this ill-reputed fish, Walker, Minnesota, has a 5K run on the ice each winter called the "Eelpout Peel Out." Mac added that up in International Falls they farm eelpout and haul them in with nets. Admirable events, yes, but the eelpout has yet to win much affection in the hearts of most ice fishermen.

Our conversation and the fishing were both slowing. I sat wondering aloud just how thick the ice was here. Mac thought it was about three feet thick. I told them about an ice fishing contest on Forest Lake I had attended. There had been 3500 holes drilled in the ice about ten feet apart in a grid pattern. Hundreds of people showed up for the event and I was in the center of the area when they handed out the prizes at the end. When I noticed water on the ice and saw water spouting up like a spring from the nearest hole because of all the weight on the ice, I decided to leave.

I realized nobody was listening to my story. Gary was snoring. Jimmy was doing the dishes. Mac was babbling, "A watched pot never boils and a watched bobber never bobs. They sometimes Bill or Chuck, but rarely bob." I was ready to go home.

Mac said it was time for the cake. All three of them hooted and yahooed. I could hear Hank's snow plow passing the fishhouse just as we finished eating the Better-Than-Sex Cake. It was a good cake, but it wasn't better than sex.

Skylights, solar panels, a patio door and TV...just like downtown

For security, put your fishhouse real close to the dock, or try ice fishing in a boat

Ice Fishing in a Boat

Duane Shodeen is the Regional Fisheries Manager for the Department of Natural Resources in Minnesota and has an office at the DNR hatchery on the Mississippi in St. Paul. He is the only guy we ever heard of who went ice fishing in a boat.

I've been going out ice fishing since the 1950s. I'd rather catch panfish than just about anything else I can think of, and sunfish are my favorite. I remember that it used to be all crappie, walleye and northern until monofilament line came along. Nobody fished seriously through the ice for sunfish until then.

I feel like I have a real advantage going out for panfish. The walleye season closes February 15th, but the panfish season is open all the time. My favorite times for ice fishing are early and late in the season when no one else is out. It's funny in Minnesota, but fishing is real popular until Labor Day and then people seem to forget about it and concentrate on hunting. For me that's the time I start planning my first ice fishing trips. Just when everyone else is wrapping it up, I like to start. I'll go out early when the ice is new before any of the houses are up and before anyone is driving on the lakes. You can really move around on the lakes then. If you want to catch fish, you have to move, you can't just sit at one hole all day. Early in the winter it is easy to drill holes all over the place because the ice is not very thick. Later on when you get thirty inches of ice you tend to stay where you are.

I go out on some pretty thin ice, but I try to be cautious. I'm never the first one to drive out on a lake, but I don't mind being the first one out walking. I wouldn't go out on a strange lake. There are some lakes that are dangerous every year. The locals stay away from them. That water is cold. When the water is thirty-nine degrees you don't have to drown to die.

I think it is far more dangerous on the first ice than on the late ice. There has to be at least ten inches of ice and a bunch of other cars before I drive out there. You hear about cars going through at the beginning of the winter but not late in the winter. I think the reason is that the ice melts around the edges of the lake first from all the dirt and salt that accumulates there, so you can't drive out on it. But you can still walk on it for another couple of weeks after it is unsafe for driving. When it gets bad close to the shore I use my hip boots to get out on it. I take my chisel with me too, and use it like a walking stick, tapping the ice in front of me before I walk on it.

I've got some friends who like to go out with me on the river bottom backwater areas of the Mississippi south of here. Some of the old river channels down there are only two feet deep and most of them not more than ten feet. The fishing is good early, right when it first freezes up. Three out of four years we can be there on Thanksgiving. I know it's south and you think that it can't be frozen that early, but the water is so shallow that all those little fingers freeze up quick. The sunny fishing is great, but it seems like the best fishing only lasts a week or two, so if you wait until you hear about it, the best fishing is going to be done and gone.

A lot of these backwater areas have a strong spring flow that comes in beneath the water surface. Since the ground water doesn't have any oxygen in it, it doesn't take long for it to push the good water out. In these shallow bay areas the fish are there at freeze-up, but a few weeks later they are forced to move out and follow the good water.

One year we went down to Wilcox Slough, and there was only an inch of ice and it wasn't thick enough to get out. There was a guy there who rented boats, and we asked him if we could rent a couple for the six of us. We split up three to a boat, and we got alongside and slid them out on the ice with us leaning on the rail and pushing them along. The boats helped to spread our weight, and they slid along like big sleds. The surface was all glare ice with no snow and you couldn't stand on it, but as long as you kept leaning and pushing on the boat you were fine. When we got out to where we wanted to fish we climbed into the boats and chopped our holes with the ice chisels and settled back to fish. A weird thing happened though: the weight of the boats with us in them pushed down on the ice, and the water came up through the fishing holes so that we were floating around in a pond on top of the ice. It was okay until we caught a fish that was too small to keep and we threw him back. The fish went swimming around the boat on top of the ice with no idea of how to find the hole to get back down into the river. So we had to take the fish that weren't keepers and push them down the hole to get them through.

When it was time to quit we used the ice chisels to push the boats out of the water and back onto the ice. Then it was out onto the ice and push them along again. That's the only time I ever went ice fishing in a boat.

The Sport of Winter Fishing

The excerpt that follows is a romantic look at ice fishing written in the florid style of the late Victorians. It's part of an article by Harry J. Ladue which appeared in the December 1, 1920 issue of Western Magazine.

To the average ardent fisherman, the "melancholy days" are epitomized by the ice-sheeted lake and the white-blanketed ground, temporarily in Jack Frost's mighty grip. He therefore, sits in a sizzling hot room gazing disconsolately through the frost-coated windows at the landscape which a few short weeks before held such tempting invitations. Verily, he hath eyes and seeth not, for if he would but don good warm clothing and plunge boldly-forth into the stinging cold he would find wholesome and satisfying vent for the energy stored up on countless summer angling excursions. And better still he may again enjoy the thrill of combat with the denizens of the waters he loves so well, albeit he must exchange the casting and fly rod for the spear and drop line. The methods employed may not seemingly have the same sporting possibilities but, believe me, there are other inducements and the fish are more delectable than at any other season.

To those who readily attune themselves to nature's varying moods, the pleasurable, invigorating snow-shoe tramp through the wonderful whiteness of the winter woods, the unaccustomed friendliness of the brave little chickadee and nut-hatch, the thrill of unraveling the trail of the fur-bearers and the breasting of the blasts sweeping across the ice-locked lakes will be sufficient unto the day thereof. While those of more materialistic mold will call the day successful which hurries them homeward in its quickly fading light with a goodly string of pickerel, perch or crappie.

Hook and line fishing through the ice and spearing fish in a fish-house are the two most popular methods of winter fishing in vogue in the inland lakes of Minnesota.

Hook and line fishing through the ice is a sport calling for stamina and endurance to the Nth degree, but a very satisfying one to the red-blooded man. The first requisite is good, warm clothing and footwear, for an hour on the bare surface of a wind-swept lake with the mercury below zero will chill you to the bone unless properly clothed. The clothing, par excellence, consists of heavy weight woolen underwear and socks, woolen outing shirt and trousers, a sweater and a parka. The parka is a north woods garment which excels all others as a windproof, loose outer covering and has a hood which can be drawn over the head.

The fishing tackle can be the same as used in your summer still-fishing, although it would be a good idea to invest in a strong line that will stand the constant friction against the ice-walls of your fishing hole. The provident fisherman will cache a supply of earthworms in his basement in the early fall for sunfish bait and I know of some who maintain a "froggery," using the green amphibians as bait for both bass and pickerel. The best all-around bait is minnow, if procurable. They can be seined in an open brook or spring or through the ice along shore if holes are cut large enough to permit the use of dip-nets. Minnows are also kept in fair-sized tanks in warm basements by some of my angling acquaintances. Taken all in all, they undoubtedly furnish the most alluring invitation to dine that you can offer the piscatorial epicure of the icy waters.

The next necessary part of your impedimenta, and you'll find on a long snow-shoe tramp that the word "impedimenta" is used advisedly, is a good axe. A leather sheath is almost a necessity for this tool, no matter how you carry it. The old rule that "an ounce of prevention is worth a pound of cure" is at no time more applicable than when carrying sharp-edged tools and especially in the woods, where the footing is never secure. You can easily strap a sheathed axe so that it can be carried on the back. You will also have need for an ice chisel and this can be made portable by taking an ordinary socket chisel and removing the handle and drilling a hole into the socket from the side. A pole can then be cut near the lake and fitted into the socket, driving a nail into the hole to make secure.

On arriving at the lake and picking the likely spot for your operations, your first task will be to cut through the ice, and here a word of advice will not be amiss. Start your hole by cutting a long gash, narrowing the hole the deeper you go. You'll thus be able to get a good swing with the axe without danger of breaking the handle or barking your knuckles as so often happens in cutting a round hole. Furthermore, you'll overcome the difficulty of lifting a solid core from the hole.

When you have chopped down to within an inch or two of the water, substitute your chisel for the axe. This is a precarious operation, for if the axe bites through and allows the hole to fill with water at the first blow you are in for a shower or your hands may lose their grip and then "good-bye" axe.

With the fishing hole properly cleaned out and your hook baited you are now ready to fish and your first catch or two will seem somewhat sluggish to your mind as you remember the snappy fighters of the good old summer time.

Later on your eyes and your thoughts will commence to concentrate on that battered old pack-sack lying in the snow, which will in turn conjure up mind pictures of the snug, wind-protected hollow nestling in the woods on the near shore with a sputtering little fire sending its curling smoke wreaths up through the bare branches. If you would enjoy all the pleasures of a real outing, on no account leave out this part of the day's program. A pot of coffee and several pork chops or strips of bacon over a winter camp fire will add perfection to your perfect day.

Fishing in a fish-house is a more elaborate method of following the gentle art and mayhaps a more appealing one to you. The fish are procured by spearing and the operations are carried on in a little darkened shack or under a blanket or snow-house set up on the ice. This is a licensed privilege to be obtained from the state game and fish commissioner upon the payment of the required fee of one dollar.

The blanket and snow-house are, of course, makeshifts and somewhat uncomfortable. They are, however, used to some extent by our northern Indians and trappers. The fish-house, if properly constructed, is about as cozy a little shelter in which to indulge in winter fishing as can be had under the circumstances. It is comparatively economical to build; in fact, is usually constructed out of odds and ends of lumber, corrugated iron, sheet iron and tin, tar-paper or manufactured paper substitutes, the chief aim being to produce a shelter about six feet in height and with floor dimensions of about four feet by four feet that will be fairly weatherproof, light-proof and light in weight. The best and most durable houses are made of matched lumber. The principal objection to corrugated or sheet iron or tin is the excessive weight. Tar-paper stretched over a wooden frame makes a very good fishing house, dark and warm and light enough to be readily moved by one man. It requires careful handling, however, as the paper tears easily. Furthermore, tools and other paraphernalia left in them are never safe, as the paper shacks are easily broken into by intruders. The manufactured material known as beaver board or composition board answers the weight requirements admirably, but it has one disadvantage and that is its susceptibility to warping and cracking under adverse weather conditions.

The roof should slant enough to insure good drainage and a fair grade of roofing paper will make the best covering for it. To facilitate moving, your house must be equipped with a pair of runners. They can be attached permanently to the foundation or to a frame upon which you can lift your house....

The first problem will be that of heating. Wood stoves, kerosene heaters and charcoal heaters are used by the majority, the above arrangement designating their relative popularity. Wood stoves are excellent heaters and the rustling of fuel for one will put no small amount of red corpuscles in your system....

The next article of furniture for your consideration will be a seat, and let me admonish you to take some care in selecting and upholstering it, because you will spend many an hour on it. The space underneath the seat can be utilized as a bin for fuel. A shelf or two built along the wall will prove handy for decoys and odds and ends in general and your own ingenuity will undoubtedly suggest other interior devices such as cupboards for dishes, etc., as they become necessary....

Remember that "it is not all of fishing to fish;" that the beauty of the winter lakes and woods, the friendly advances of the cheery, little winter birds and the stimulating activity in the pure winter air are as essential to your complete enjoyment of the sport as the mere procuring of fish. The sport of winter fishing has all the attractiveness of any angling and will make you healthy in body, wealthy in memories and wise in new and interesting ways of enjoying our sparkling northern waters.

A Pour House Fish

David Tripp is secretary of the Siren, Wisconsin Lion's Club. This is his story of the Lion's Club winter activities on Clam Lake.

I'm from Georgia, and if you'd told me a few years ago that I'd be driving my car onto the middle of a frozen lake at ten below zero to go fishing, I'd have told your you were crazy. But here I am. This is my third year in the Lion's Club and my second year at the annual ice fishing party. Most of the kids from town are here.

The 24-hole Lion's Club Fishhouse is our headquarters, but most of the time it's our concession stand. Next month, for the Sixteenth Annual Waterskip we move it to the north end of the lake and sell hot dogs and beer out of it.

The Waterskip is our major fund raising event of the year. When the weather is nice, as many as ten thousand people come to see snowmobiles drag racing. It's a big thing these days; there is actually a professional circuit of International Snowmobile Waterskippers with events all over the world. The snowmobiles skip right on top of channels of open water, and if they can keep up their momentum, they don't sink.

The Waterskip doesn't happen until the last week in February, so we still have a month to get ready. Today's fishing party is paid for with funds assessed from the members in 25-cent fines collected at our bimonthly meetings for such offenses as not wearing the official hat and vest, arriving late or failing to address a fellow Lion without using the honorific "Lion" before his name. Insults, whether they are real, imagined or made up, are usually good for a quarter as well.

Today we've got our outdoor kitchen going. They're using the bonfire in the wheelbarrow for keeping warm and they're stoking up the big grills to cook the "brats" and hot dogs. The kids will be running around like this all day chasing each other and running down the flags from their tip-ups. We plan to stand here and tell fish stories and sip beer around the fire.

The kids get prizes for everything they catch, but most of them don't take it too seriously. In fact, we have to remind them that the flags are up, or they would forget all about it. Usually we plow up a big pile of snow for them to play on, but the ice was bare this year; there wasn't enough snow to bother with.

The hardest duty on fishing day is making the awards. It seems most of the hammer-handle northerns in this lake are twin brothers and sisters, because they all come out about the same size. Last year they had a devil of a time deciding who caught which fish and whose was bigger. From what I have seen so far, I think we are going to have the same trouble today.

Usually when I go out ice fishing with Butch and his dad, Merle, and Gary Lund, we take a twelve-pack and stay until the beer's gone or until someone catches a decent fish. The first time I ever went ice fishing was with Gary. We sat for two hours on this lake in northern Wisconsin with a ten-below blizzard buffeting the house. No one said a word. We just stared at our bobbers and watched the whiteout. Gary finally said, "It don't get no better than this." When we finish the beer or someone catches a decent fish (a five- or six-pounder) we go uptown to the Pour House and have one. Of course most of the time the "twelver's" gone before we get a suitable Pour House fish, but we go to the Pour House anyway.

At last year's fishing party, Ronnie Yourchuck got a major fine for stealing a kid's fish. It was a big one, like a ten-pounder. He had caught it right at the end of the day. Everyone says that Ronnie wrestled it away from the kid. I wasn't there, but it must have been pretty funny.

The guys all took it right down to the Pour House. Even though it was stolen, it was definitely a Pour House fish. Ron'd had a couple I suppose. Well, three anyway. He walked into the Pour House, which was jammed with people, and he had this big old snake slung over his shoulder. He flopped it down on the floor and everyone cheered and it was drinks all around. One of the guys sitting there, said, "That ain't nothing." He went out to his truck and brought in a twelve-pound walleye and threw it on the floor. I guess that went over so well they went to three or four other places in town and pulled the same stunt. I'm real sorry I missed it.

A suitable Pour House catch

The dignity and grace of a fishouse rental unit

The Teepee

At the <u>Fish and Eat</u> restaurant in a small town in Lake County, Illinois, the proprietor told this story about the county sportsman's club.

Ice fishing? I love ice fishing. A couple of years ago 250 people went from here on an ice fishing trip to a pay-by-the-inch trout pond in Wisconsin. It was a terrific crowd. All the members of the Lake County Sportsman Club brought their parents, grandparents, uncles, aunts, children and grandchildren. My wife and I took the two oldest kids, and it was a big time just driving up there.

When we arrived we drilled a lot of holes and the kids got to do a lot of fishing. It was colder than it gets around here, but the kids didn't pay any attention to it. The older guys, though, didn't think much of fishing on the bare ice. They were enjoying themselves; part of the fun was ribbing the younger people about freezing their private parts.

Well, some of them were old Swedes and they had come prepared, though the rest of us didn't know it. They started hauling tarps and 2x4s and tools and ropes out of a couple of the pickup trucks and the rest of us wondered what was going on. Before long they had fastened all this stuff together, and they had a giant teepee put up where a bunch of them could fish together and get out of the cold. At one point I counted ten of them in there. It looked a little strange since the pond wasn't very big, but they didn't care what it looked like.

They had brought an oil heater which they turned up full blast, and it got so warm inside that it started to melt the ice. Soon they were splashing around in two or three inches of water. The younger guys asked if they were trying to melt the whole lake, but those old Swedes were so happy that they didn't notice a thing. The water turned into a small pond that extended several feet beyond the tent, but they weren't worried about it.

Late in the afternoon they ran out of fuel oil, and, as the temperature dropped, the water turned back into ice. Before long the bottom of the teepee was frozen solid, and the 2x4s and tarps were locked into the pond. The owner of the trout farm said there was no way they were going to leave their teepee behind, and they had better get it out.

So they chopped this thing out of the ice. They were using hammers, tire irons, chisels, axes and whatever they happened to have along. It took about two hours and all the young people were teasing them the whole time.

Here's the sled that has a convertible top you can pull up over your head to cover you and your fishing hole

The Reverend Roger's High-Tech Ice Fishing Package

Last summer we stopped at a big sporting goods shop in St. Paul to see if we could take pictures of some ice fishing equipment. Since it was June, the ice fishing goodies had long since been packed away in the basement, and the manager had to bring them all back upstairs. During the ensuing confusion, Roger, one of the salesmen and a professional fishing guide, talked to us.

"What are you telling people about ice fishing?" he asked.

"What do you mean?"

"You don't want to give people the wrong idea," he said.

"We're just passing along some of the ice fishing stories we've heard."

"Yes, but what if someone reads this book and then tries to go ice fishing without any experience? They could get off to a bad start without the right stuff."

"The right stuff?"

"Yes, it's important to have the right equipment."

Roger turned out to be an evangelist for The Right Equipment. We told him right there in the store we were going to have to call him the Reverend Roger. He laughed and began to talk so fast the tape recorder could barely keep up. We pointed to the four-dollar jigging rods and the plastic tip-ups.

"No way," he said. "You need one of these little graphite beauties."

"But those rods are thirty-two bucks apiece" we said. "Part of the charm of this sport is that you can do it without investing a lot of money."

He picked up a fancy Japanese spinning reel, "And you should have a reel like this one."

"What's wrong with a plastic spool and some monofilament line?"

"Be serious," he said. He was laying out a couple of hundred dollars worth of jigs he thought absolutely essential.

"What about a package of hooks, a bobber and some minnows?" We felt that someone had to speak for the thousands of fishermen of modest means.

"No way," he said. "Come over to my house and I'll show you what you need."

We followed Roger to his place. When we got there we suggested setting the equipment up on the lawn so we could take a couple of pictures and see how it all went together. He had a 3x4-foot molded fiberglass sled with high sides and a bench across the front. It had a canvas convertible top you could pull over you and your fish hole when you were out on a freezing-cold day. He had a gas heater, a case of jigs for every lake and every day of the week, a fancy power auger and a stainless steel ice scooper to clear the hole. He had a gas lantern and several different graphite rods. (See Photo Glossary, page 131.)

We took turns sitting on the sled and pulling the top up. We tried the action on all his graphite rods and asked him, "Is all this really necessary?"

"Every bit of it. Do you want to be a successful ice fisherman?" He opened up the case of his electronic fish finder.

"That too?"

"You bet. I've ice fished on hundreds of different lakes and this is the only way to go."

We talked some more and asked Roger for his best fish stories, but every time he started telling one, he got sidetracked on the piece of equipment involved. Roger was a salesman and a teacher. We wanted another good fish story, but he wanted to do a workshop on ice fishing.

"This is not a how-to book," we told him. "We just want to hear about what happens out there on the ice. We are as interested in the 'wrong stuff' as the 'right stuff.'"

But True Evangelist Roger was more interested in keeping us from going astray than he was in telling stories. He did tell us about falling through the ice one time, but the whole point of his story was that he was wearing his springtime ice fisherman flotation device, and he popped right back to the surface before the guy walking beside him even missed him. When we pressed him for more details he brought out the vest, pointed out its best features - it was light, efficient and stylish - and showed us a pair of spikes joined by a long length of cord that you should also carry on the ice. The spikes dangle out of your sleeves and the cord goes up the arms and around your shoulders inside your shirt. The idea is that when you fall in, you can grab these spikes and use them to pull yourself up onto the ice.

"That would be great to have."

"It's not just having the equipment, but knowing how to use it that counts."

"You're a great salesman, and we'd buy it all if we had the money."

We thanked the Reverend Roger for taking the time to drag everything onto the lawn, and we promised to call if we ever did a book on the right stuff for ice fishermen.

Bad Timing

In Minnesota you can't lock the door to your fishhouse when you're fishing, and the game warden has the right to bust right in whenever he thinks you might be breaking the law. That's the fishing law of course. Since fishhouses have become so comfortable, and since the fishing room also doubles as the bedroom, and since many ice fishers like to have their significant others with them on a frosty winter night, opening the door can still lead to some embarrassing moments. This is the story of Larry's most poorly-timed ice fishing interview.

It was during my first trip to Mille Lacs Lake that I found a two-story fishhouse with a bright orange door, and, thinking it had a couple of good stories, I knocked on the door. I wasn't sure if I should knock my second knock or leave, when the door opened a crack. I said I was writing a book on ice fishhouses and ice fishing stories and that I wanted to talk to them. With a smile, he said, "Come on in, that's a subject that I've been thinking of writing about." Inside, he started talking as he looked around for something that he may have been doing before I knocked. His wife started washing a clean frying pan and acted like she was bored. She had a 'guilty-as-hell' smile. It was obviously poor timing on my part.

"I'm Frank and this is my wife Susan. What do you want to know?"

I asked him to tell me about his house and what he does there.

Frank pointed out the triangular shape on the top of the house that was a sleeping loft, so I climbed up the ladder to look. Susan pointed out the nice picture window and laughed self-consciously. Frank said the design was all wrong and that it got too hot up there.

Was he trying to tell me something?

Then he said that there was a fifteen-foot hump under the water. A hump is another term for reef or sandbar. We looked at the fishing holes in the floor and we looked at the fishing rods. "There are plenty of walleye on this hump. I found them with the locater, but they haven't been biting for about a month. Right now we are catching a lot of perch. It's nice being out here by ourselves." I had already stayed longer than I should have.

I noticed that Susan was still cleaning the frying pan as Frank talked about the LORAN C unit he was going to buy so that in the wintertime he could re-find the summertime fishing spots. The LORAN C is another electronic gadget which uses a navigational satellite triangulation system to locate any place you would want to re-find. It stores the coordinates for that spot in its data bank along with the information for about fifty other memorable places. It's one more weapon in the electronic battle with the fish.

He told me about a company that hauls fishermen out to the middle of Mille Lacs Lake in track vehicles which are similar to the WWII half-tracks. They use 8x8 portable aluminum fishouses, pulling seven or eight of them at a time and they have the fishing spots punched into the memory of their LORAN unit, so they don't have to search for a good spot each time.

"Some things I do would be good to put in your book. I don't know if other people know about them or not, but they are good ideas. One thing I do is dig out the ends of the cabin when I leave at the end of the weekend. It lets the cold air get under the place so that the holes will freeze over again. If you just leave the snow banked up, the solar energy the cabin stores is enough to keep the holes from freezing, which isn't a problem unless there is a big snow while you are gone. If you get four-foot drifts all around the cabin, with that extra weight pushing down on the ice and water coming up through the holes, you're likely to come back to a cabin with a thick ice floor."

I told him I liked his fishouse design and as Susan's frying pan got cleaner, Frank talked about how he would build his next fishouse.

"My next fishouse will have a barn-style roof, double loft with two bedrooms upstairs, about ten by eighteen, and twelve feet tall at the peak. Probably cost me three to five thousand dollars. It gets expensive when you start getting into the little extras. Windows that cost almost $2000 to put in a fishouse? It's ridiculous.

"There's a fishouse on the lake that cost $30,000 to build, but it's so heavy that they don't even haul it out on the ice anymore. It has four fireplaces."

I was hoping for something more in the line of stories than fishing facts, but I enjoyed my visit with them. When I left, I noticed that the frying pan was hanging on the wall, sparkling clean. Susan was sitting on the couch and Frank was looking at her with a smile. The long wait at the beginning, the frying pan scene, holes, humps, rods, hot bedrooms - maybe she should have hit me with the frying pan. I guess the story was there all along.

Right landscape, wrong shelter. Those aren't fish bones over the door, either

Appropriately located near Liberty Beach on Mille Lacs Lake, MN

Fly Fishing on Ice

I met him in a restaurant in Michigan's upper peninsula and we talked about ice fishing while we ate bacon and eggs. We were sitting at the counter all alone. He was probably in his eighties, and he was dressed to go ice fishing, even though fishing of any kind was now only a memory.

"You heard about the two guys sitting out on the ice and a hearse drove by?" I didn't tell him that I had heard it several years earlier in Chicago with the main characters being golfers instead of fishermen. "Well, what happened was the one guy stood up and took off his hat and stood there. When he sat back down and picked up his fishing pole, the other guy said: 'That was nice of you,' and he said, 'Well, she was a good wife for thirty-five years.'"

He went on talking, glancing at me occasionally to see if I was listening. "I used to have four shanties and I kept each one on a different lake. I used one as a darkhouse for spearing jack. One we would take out on the big lake and use when we fished for lakers. One I used to fish for walleye and the other one was for perch and crappies. I would try to go to a different shanty each day, but if the fishing was great in one of them, I would always end up back at that shanty the next day. You never got bored when the fishing was good. You know why the Finns don't ice fish?"

"No."

"It takes them too long to chop the hole for their boat."

"Okay, so tell me more about your ice fishing days," I said, guessing that he wasn't a Finn.

"Well, once I was fishing with a friend on Lake Superior and we left to go get lunch. While we were gone, the wind changed direction. When we got back, the ice we had been fishing on was gone. The wind had blown it out to sea. I think about that a lot. What if we hadn't gotten hungry?

"Another time my friend Henry was with some guys out on Lake Superior and they were catching lots of lake trout through the ice about a mile from shore. I found out about it and went out to fish with them. When I got there, the ice had broken off and drifted out on the big lake. I saw them out there waving and all. I called the Coast Guard and they sent a boat out to get them."

"Sounds like they were stranded on an oversized ice cube, huh?"

"Yeah... One time I was ice fishing and I caught a real big walleye and this guy watching me came over and told me he had caught a bigger one in the same hole the year before."

"Really?"

"That was a joke; don't you get it?"

I said, "Oh yeah, that's funny," but I still didn't get it for another couple of minutes. When I did get it I decided it was my turn. "Did you know that the Montanans are always making fun of the North Dakotans?" He didn't, but I went ahead anyway. "A guy from Montana told me about a North Dakotan who was fly fishing on the ice. Another North Dakotan rode up to him on his snowmobile and asked if he was catching any. The fly fisherman said 'No,' and the other guy said, 'Hop on the back of the snowmobile and you can troll for awhile.'"

I knew he liked that one because he started looking around for someone he could tell it to. That was my cue. I told him I enjoyed talking to him. I was off to find another ice fishing story somewhere down the road.

Could it be David Letterman?

Fishtown 1878

Over one hundred years ago Frank Leslie's Illustrated Newspaper *ran a story called "Fishtown." When we found it in the historical collection at Central Michigan University, we realized two things: first, it was obvious that fishhouses were being used for more than spearing long before World War II; and second, the fishhouse "villages" that we found so intriguing were not really a new phenomenon after all. Here's the article as it appeared in the February 16, 1878 edition. The original title was, "A Winter Settlement on the Ice in Saginaw Bay, on Lake Huron."*

On the borders of Lake Huron, where its waters dash up against the thickly wooded shores of the State of Michigan, is an inlet known as Saginaw Bay. Visit this inlet any time before the long Winter sets in, and you will see the bay dotted over with innumerable fishing boats, whose white sails resemble so many graceful sea-gulls skimming over the water; in these boats are the fishermen dragging their nets for Mackinaw trout.

Hundreds support themselves in this way through the season when the lake and bay are free from ice; but a time soon comes when, for twenty miles out from the shore, an ice bridge forms; thick enough to sustain a whole village, and the mercury seldom rising above zero from the last of November until the first of March, the fishermen and their families would be quite destitute as soon as the bleak Winter commences, had not a mode been established whereby they could fish all the Winter through. As there was no work to be accomplished, there was, of course, much suffering, and an opportunity offered to prove the proverb that "necessity is the mother of invention." Many ways were devised, and much cogitating racked the minds of the poor, until they at last concluded to try the experiment of each man's building himself a house and moving it on to the lake, directly the ice formed. It was no sooner thought of than put to the test, and several hundred families moved out from shore, and by cutting a larger square hole through the solid floor into the dark waters, they were enabled to drop their nets and secure the fish.

It seems almost incredible that it is possible for so large a number of people to live at once upon the ice; but is a favorite haunt of Jack Frost, and he comes puffing and blowing from his home in the Spitzbergen regions with a blast that not only bites fingers and noses and tingles ears with a cruel nip, but keeps a solid foundation for the ice city for many months.

If you never have been upon the shores of Lake Huron in mid-Winter, you never have felt truly cold weather. The renown of this curious city reached us long before we were willing to accept the truth of the report, and it was not until we had visited it and beheld the markets and green groceries, the odd little-log-dwellings containing only one room, with a stove perched upon a shelf to prevent the ice from melting, and had peeped through the large square hole in the floor where the men were dragging in the fish, could we believe such a city really existed - scarcely even then could we feel certain that it was not a myth, or a fairy village, that would soon slip away and leave, where were now roads and houses, taverns and markets, but angry treacherous waters that would bear not a trace of the hundreds of busy workmen so recently living above them.

Ice fishing villages haven't really changed much since 1878

The houses are built on wheels, much after the fashion of a photographer's portable house; have a door and a chimney, are furnished with very little comfort, and generally contain from four to five people in each. The village lies ten miles from shore and includes, besides the large number of dwellings, many markets and stores. We did not expect to see so many happy faced people in such a dreary, desolate place; possibly it might have been because of the unusual excitement that prevailed at the good fortune of bringing in a ten pound trout, or it might be owing to the clear Western climate, that we beheld so many sturdy people; but, I take it, it would be quite impossible to find a city lad who could outstrip a Michigan boy in a long run - here he thinks no more of skating twelve miles to shore and back than of walking two city blocks on a frosty morning. The clear atmosphere is invigorating and healthful, such a disease as pulmonary complaint never having been known. Once, two fishermen more venturous than the rest, remained a night too long in the fast-ebbing village, and in the morning not a trace of ice could be seen beyond the small cake on which they floated; fortune, however, served them a good turn, for, after floating in the lake for two days and nights, a cold east-wind prevailed which was sufficient to form a new bridge, and upon this they skated ashore. The lives of the inhabitants are thus fraught with danger, as a sudden change in the temperature may leave them at any time without their city; therefore, it seems to present a constant fluctuation, and the owners of the cabins, not being burdened with much furniture, are ever ready to close their doors and at a moment's notice drag their families to terra firma. But this does not often happen, as Jack Frost's visits are generally so prolonged as to leave no doubt regarding the safety of the city. It seemed to us, who were unaccustomed to so cheerless an existence, that the living in such a bleak, dreary town must of necessity be very demoralizing; but we found the men and boys enjoying themselves with cards, spinning yarns and singing in a very sailorly manner, and apparently enjoying life as much as "lubberly landsmen." Christmas is celebrated, too, in these humble dwellings, and we found scarcely a house undecorated with a bit of pine and holly, the inmates rejoicing over the day Christ was born with as much real enjoyment as though they could celebrate the Advent with gifts befitting the wealthiest.

The fishermen find their employment almost as profitable in Winter as in the Spring and Summer, and haul twice a day. The nets are sunk with weights and stretched to their uttermost, being fastened to sticks laid across the opening in the ice. The hardy sons of the ice seem far more contented with their mode of living than we could imagine possible, and are a far better class of men than the gangs who hew timber in the Michigan forests, to be floated down the rivers in the Spring to the lumber-mills that line the Saginaw River. The road that leads to Fishtown carries the traveler through many tracts of unbroken snow and across plains and desolate country. The wind was blowing a steady gale during our day-journey in the family sleigh, and made us well wish to shorten the fifteen miles of travel, before we stepped upon the frozen bay, after which we must still ride ten miles before reaching the phantom city. But in due time it was accomplished, and we beheld what we have already described. The vicinity of Fishtown, upon the shore, is wild and uninviting-looking, and we were glad enough to turn our faces homeward, to find a warm, cheerful fire to welcome us, congratulating ourselves that the perilous journey need not be again repeated, and grateful that our lives lay in pleasanter places than these of the fishermen whom we had just visited, ten miles out upon the ice.

Twee Flesk Nappa Best

I found Ray Hendrickson ice fishing for perch in February on a lake in upstate New York. Ray told me about his background. He said that his father still lived on the old homestead in Jamestown, was active in the Swedish Salvation Army and received a card from the King and Queen of Sweden for his one-hundredth birthday. I was afraid that being one-half Swede was not going to be enough to get Ray's trust and keep his attention, so I lied about my heritage and claimed to be 100 percent Swedish. That's the only lie in this chapter. Honest.

When I met him, Ray was fishing for perch, sunfish and bluegills on Canadaigua. As usual it was slow that day. It seemed that everywhere I went that winter I had missed the greatest fishing by forty-eight hours or so. In this same spot just a week earlier he had fished for less than an hour, and caught over fifty keeper-perch.

Ray fished with his bobber beneath the surface. "I'll tell you how it works. The sinker's on the bottom and I have a lead line running off it that keeps the bobber under the water. That's so the wind can't blow it around. When those fish hit sometimes they will just barely touch it, and if the bobber is on the top, the wind will blow it around and you can't tell if you've had a bite or a puff of wind. This way you have a little better idea of what's going on."

He told me that Canadaigua was good for lake trout. In the summer, a friend of his goes out in a boat and gets his limit in two or three hours every day. He also told me that Chautauqua Lake over by Jamestown was the muskie capital of the world. But after somebody put walleye in, it became a walleye lake. He never told me where the new muskie capital was.

He wanted to know if my forefathers were from Sweden. I said that my grandparents were but I didn't know a word of Swedish and I wondered what the words painted on his fishing box meant. They read, "Twee Flesk Nappa Best," and I took a picture so I would be sure to get it right. He said that they use pork for bait in Sweden and that the saying is, "Spit on the pork and the fish will bite the best." Ray said he'd got all the grandkids to spit on their bait just like the old Swedes.

"You actually spit on your bait? I always thought you weren't even supposed to touch your hook."

"That's what they did in the old country."

I asked some Swedes in town about "twee flesk nappa best" and none of them understood. Harold Tangren in Lindstrom, Minnesota, said that when he grew up the saying was "Spit on the hook," but it didn't sound anything like the words on Ray's tackle box. Harold also said that his father-in-law told him that they used pork in Denmark to fish for eels. They just tied it on a string and the eels were so greedy that they hung on even when you pulled them out of the water.

"Yes, but does this spitting really work?" I asked.

"You bet it does. One time I caught a fifteen-pound muskie. It was the biggest fish I ever caught through the ice, but I had to throw it back because it wasn't in season."

"That's a big fish."

"That's not the half of it."

"What do you mean?"

"Are you really Swedish?"

I assured him again that I was.

"Well, then I can tell you this."

"Do you mean if I weren't Swedish you wouldn't tell me?"

"Well, this way I think you will really understand. I was fishing for perch when I caught the muskie."

"And you spit on the bait?" I asked.

"Yes, I spit on the bait, and I caught me a nice little perch but when I was pulling it in, *wham!* something grabbed it from under the ice. It was the muskie and I just pulled them in together."

"A fifteen-pounder and you threw it back?"

"Yep," he said seriously, and stared at the hole in the ice.

"What part of Sweden are your grandparents from?" he asked.

"Near Malmo," I said and hoped there was such a place in Sweden.

"Then, I'll tell you something else," he said.

"About spitting on your bait?" I asked

"Nope. This is something that happened in a fishhouse."

"Do I have to be Swedish to appreciate it?"

"No, but I think it helps."

"What happened?"

"Well, I had the frying pan all greased up on the stove and the fat was smoking and it was ready to go. I caught a nice perch, and I flipped him up on the table and cut off a fillet and popped it in the pan. When I turned back to the table to get the second side, the fish took one look at me and jumped off the table, took a couple of flops across the floor and dived right back down the hole."

"Are you kidding?"

"With one-half of it still swimming in the lake, it was the freshest fish I ever ate."

A couple of weeks after I got home from New York there was a letter from Ray. He said the fishing had gotten better again a couple of days after he saw me on Canadaigua, and he sent along a batch of great pictures of ice fishing taken in the 50s. He also said that I could use any of his stories because he didn't mind sharing them, one Swede to another.

It's nothing fancy, but it does the trick

Special Delivery?

The Trout Pond

It's Highway 23 in Massachusetts, a diversion from the interstate. The fifth lake that Larry comes to, Little Bend Pond, has a bunch of fishermen on it. One of them is pulling a plastic sled full of tip-up units, reels, jigs, hooks, thermos bottles and paper bags.

"Catch any fish?"

"Yeah, a few."

"What do they normally catch in here?"

"Well, they got trout, uh **perch**, in here, and bass."

"It's a deep lake then, huh?"

"Yeah, deep enough for perch."

"I thought you said there were trout."

"Perch and bass, mostly perch."

"You like trout fishing?"

"Yeah, some."

"So how often do you come here?"

"Oh, I was here a couple of days ago. I like it. It's close and the trou...the perch ain't too bad. You an ice fisherman?"

"Do they put fishouses out here? I guess you call them bobs."

"Naw, they don't put no shanties down, they just come out here and fish. You looking for trout?"

"No, I was wondering if this ice is safe to walk on."

"Christ, yes, you got about twelve, fifteen inches out there or better. You got your fishing gear in your car?"

"I'm from Minnesota. I'm doing research on ice fishing."

"You from the government? This is a good perch lake. Why do you want to know about trout?"

"How long have you been ice fishing?"

"For years, since I was a kid."

"Is this the lake you usually fish in?"

"I like this lake. The bass, er, the perch ain't too bad. You got an out of state license? Go to Russell pond, you get trout but they're not very big."

"Do you like trout?"

"Yes, but I'd rather fish here for perch. Trout's not much good here. You've got to go north. The trout fishing is good in those lakes."

"What you got there in the sled?"

"My new auger."

"Any fish?"

"Couple of nice perch."

"Can I take a picture of them for my research?"
"Naw, I've got them all wrapped up."
"So what's a good bait for a perch?"
"A 'poich' eye."
"A perch eye?"
"Yes, you catch a small perch and stick its eye on the hook of a Swedish pimple."
"And that works?"
"Like magic. It enhances the bait."
"And does that work for trout too?"
"I've got to be getting. I've got to check on my fishing partner; she's got a sprained ankle."
"She?"
"Yeah, my wife; she's mad because she had to stay home."
"You coming back tomorrow?"
"Probably not."
"There won't be much ice fishing left this year if this warm weather keeps up."
"No. And we won't have any maple syrup either."

This gives new meaning to the term "camper"

Larry Sells a Book

In early February of a recent winter Larry drove across the north country from Minnesota to Massachusetts puddle jumping from one ice fishing lake to the next. He stopped at Oneida Lake just north of Syracuse, New York to see if anyone was catching anything.

When I pulled into Oneida I spotted a plumbing contractor's truck with a couple of guys in it taking a snooze. I slammed my door and the big guy behind the wheel woke up. When he saw me aiming my camera toward the fishermen on the ice, he rolled down his window and asked what was going on. I told him that I was taking pictures and interviewing people for a book on ice fishing, and he said I should talk to Neal Webber because he was the resident expert on ice fishing. I explained that I was from Minnesota and that I was just passing through so I didn't have much time to look for Mr. Webber. He said that there was a good chance that Neal was out there right now since he rarely missed a day of fishing and Oneida was his favorite lake.

There weren't any fishing structures on Oneida, but the ice was covered with fishermen. I started out for the closest fishing hole which looked to be a couple of hundred yards out, thinking that it would be a real piece of luck to find someone like Neal Webber.

It didn't take two minutes for my feet and the bottom of my jeans to get soaked. The ice was covered with a six-inch layer of slush with a thin layer of ice on top of that, and I soon lost track of the number of times I fell in up to my ankles. I should have taken the time to change out of my tennis shoes before I started out.

An old man was returning to shore and he stopped to chat. When I asked if he had caught anything, he showed me seven perch. I asked about the walleye fishing. "Oh Yeah! There are some nice walleye in here. Usually they catch a lot, but not this year." I asked him if he knew Neal Webber, and he said that he was Neal Webber. I told Neal that the guy in the plumbing truck had told me that he was the resident expert on ice fishing.

"He did? That's a joke. He knows more about ice fishing than anyone in the state of New York. That's my son-in-law; he's waiting for me. I think he was pulling your leg."

"Well, why isn't he out here fishing?"

"He's supposed to be working, but I talked him into picking me up on his way back from lunch."

"Do you think he would tell me some fishing stories?"

"Clarence? I doubt it. He's not much of a talker."

"There's nothing wrong with his sense of humor," I said as I started walking further away from shore and Neal continued his walk toward Clarence's truck.

Going out on the ice after fishing stories is a lot like fishing. You have to try to figure where the good stories are and you have to try to keep from getting skunked. With all those fishermen out there, I felt the odds were in my favor as long as I kept moving, so I walked on toward that first fishing hole. The guy fishing there offered me a five-gallon bucket to sit on. He had four perch that he was keeping in a hole drilled into the top of the ice, and he caught three more while I was watching.

"There is no way to figure fish out," he said.

"I guess you are right."

"I come to this same spot every week and sometimes I kill them and sometimes I just get cold feet."

"Some people have fish radar units that see under the ice," I said.

"More toys for the rich people. They don't catch any more fish."

"What's the biggest fish you ever caught out here?"

"It was a lawyer."

"What's a lawyer?"

"It's a kind of an ugly fish in the cod family that curls around your arm like a snake, but it's good eating."

"Oh, you mean an eelpout."

"No, I mean a lawyer."

I was still pretty sure that he was talking about an eelpout. Given that most people I had talked to don't want to land them because they are so ugly and slimy, I figured that this was just New York's lawyer-insulting joke.

I decided to try one more fisherman before heading back to shore. This guy's thermal long john tops were showing under the light windbreaker he was wearing unzipped. He was working one hole with a jigging stick. He told me that in New York any fishing pole is considered a tip-up if it has the fisherman's name written on it.

"What is that metal thing at the end of your pole?"

"It's called a floating bobber." The line went through a hole on the end of a small piece of spring steel attached near the end of his pole.

"When the fish bites, the spring bends toward the pole and I know that I've got a fish."

I scanned the horizon.

"You looking for someone?" the fisherman asked.

"Not really," I said, and I told him how Clarence the plumber had set me up back there in the parking lot. That got him started on a bunch of jokes about Governor Coumo of New York. When he ran out of Coumo stories he started in on Rockefeller. I tried to get him back to ice fishing, but the closest he came was to tell me that Coumo was holding up the funds for a new walleye hatchery in the area. I asked him if he had heard of any of these lakes that had so many fishhouses on them that they named the streets, formed municipalities, elected mayors and had pizza delivered. He said he had heard of a lake in New Hampshire like that. I told him that I'd heard about some in Minnesota and Michigan.

"Pretty soon they will have a McDonald's on the ice in one of those places," he said.

"If they do, they'll have to serve walleye and perch," I said.

The sun had warmed things up enough so that it was really a nice afternoon, but it also continued to warm the ice, and I fell through twice as often on the way back. One time my shoe came off. I was almost off the lake when I went through the slush half way to my knees.

Back at the parking lot Clarence and his father-in-law were gone. I got some dry socks and shoes out of the back of the truck and put them on. As I started to get into the front seat, I noticed a card under the windshield wiper. It was a business card from Clarence the plumber, and on the back he had scrawled, "Send us the book when it's done."

This one registered a 3.5 on the "Richter Pressure-Ridge Scale"

Falling In

Lou runs a used fishing gear and repair shop out of his house in Reading, Massachusetts. When he was in high school a football accident cost him his right leg. He describes the following ice fishing incident as it happened to him in New Hampshire in 1989.

Have you ever been on the ice when the pressure ridge starts to push up and the ice trembles for a minute and a half? Well, we were last year. Paul and I were on the lake, and we broke through when there was twenty inches of solid ice. The pressure ridge came up right in front of us about a foot and a half high. We were lucky this was a small one. We've seen them go as high as twelve or fifteen feet.

It was up at Merrymeeting Lake, about three A.M. when we were driving out to fish. (We always do our best fishing in the early morning or late at night.) We had had a lot of snow with maybe two or three feet on the ground followed by a warm spell and some rain. All the snow melted and the rain and everything pushed down on the ice, and, of course, while the ice is making, she is expanding and pushing up on the shore and she has to give some place, and this was the place. We felt the ice racking, trembling like an earthquake. One side was actually pressing down and sliding against the other. When it gave, it was like the rug got pulled out from under us and there was a hell of a noise. Where the ice went up it created a big hollow. There was three feet of water with eight or ten inches of ice underneath and then nothing but 130 feet of frigid lake.

So here we were driving along on twenty inches of solid ice in the pickup truck in the pitch black and there was this grinding and cracking and we were going through. We tried to open the doors and the water poured in. Our camp was only ten minutes down the road, but the ice was deserted because everyone else had hauled ass out of there earlier. Usually it was so quiet you could hear a pin drop. I loved it. A guy a mile up the lake would be talking and it was just like he was right beside you. Well, that pressure ridge went off like a cannon. Even though we were half a mile out, the people came running out of their camps.

Now Paul had his brand-new ATV in the back and I had my brand-new auger, and then we had a brand-new 35mm camera with gadgets. We knew that once you put your vehicle on the ice you voided your insurance policy. Not only do you void your insurance, but in New Hampshire and Massachusetts there is a thousand dollar a day fine for every day you leave your vehicle in the water, and they enforce it strictly. See, this lake tests as the purest in the state of New Hampshire, and they don't want a truck down there leaking gas into the water.

Well, the truck starts settling in and Paul can't get his door open, and he climbs over me and jams my door open, and he gets out onto the solid ice. But my wooden leg is caught under the seat, and the truck is still slowly going down and I'm saying, "Oh, Jesus, no." So he grabs a hold of me and he drags me out and pulls the leg out. My leg is half off and dragging behind me on the ice. We look back at the truck which has slowed down but still looks like it's sinking and we're saying, "It's going! It's going!" Well, the whole thing tipped over toward the driver's side up to the bumpers, and then it just hung there on that eight or ten inches of ice below the top layer. She was in three feet of water.

Acting like resourceful New Hampshire people, we said, "Let's go get the tow truck." But the guy with the tow truck won't come out, so we find a guy with a backhoe who will. He looks at the truck and says, "You damn fools. You shouldn't have been out there." He wouldn't take his rig out there, but he's got the biggest come-along that I've ever seen in my life and a couple of big timbers about five or six feet tall. He took my auger and went about fifteen or twenty feet behind the truck where the ice was good, and he put two holes in and set the timbers in the holes, and he wrapped the chain around one timber and then the other. Paul had to go in and hook the chain under the bumper on the ass-end and then he cranked it onto solid ice. Paul got in the truck, turned it over once, and it started right up and we drove off.

We really haven't gotten over the effects of that little experience. Even when there is thirty inches of ice and we're driving around and we hear that *crack, bump, snap* and *pop*, we grab for the door handles. We did go back out the very next morning though, and we caught some nice trout, early, half-past five, quarter to six. We drove out like we always did and sat on the back of the truck to fish.

When we got all set up, Paul said, "I'm gonna go up and see where we went through." We were at what is called the narrows. I couldn't see him the whole time he was gone because he was around the bend, but when he came back he said there was a guy fishing right where we went through.

Paul said, "This guy has a tip-up on one side of where we went in and another tip-up on the other side."

Paul had stopped the ATV, and the guy said, "You want something?"

Paul said no and the guy said, "Then what are you looking for?"

"I'm just looking at where we went through the ice last night with my truck."

The guy said, "You what?"

Now, when you go through the ice these little chunks fly out all over the place, and it looks like a debris field. Paul showed the debris to the guy. The area where the truck had gone through had about an inch of ice on it, and he had come **that** close to walking on it. He was luckier than we were.

Bringing it all back home

A camper for all seasons

The Torpedo

Mike sells photographic equipment and supplies such as cameras, enlargers, film and developer. Every weekend for the last twenty-eight winters he has gone ice fishing. He usually fishes alone because he deals with people all day, every day, and wants some solitude by the end of the week. There have been times when he's caught his limit of fish, and other times he's been skunked, but he has always gone back out the next weekend either way.

Stories? Oh yeah, one. Once I was ice fishing up north on Moose Lake, near the Moose River inlet. It was late enough in the season that most people were thinking that opening day of fishing wasn't too far away. The ice was still ten inches thick over eight to ten feet of water that was clear like you wouldn't believe, as clear as a Sierra Nevada mountain lake. I was fishing with a jigging stick and since the fish weren't biting, I dropped the pole and lay down to see what was on the other side of the ice.

All the snow that had covered the ice earlier in the season had melted and the ice was almost as clear as the water below. The sun was shining through, so I could see all the way down to where three big perch hung suspended close to the bottom. It was as though they weren't real. It reminded me at the time of a television picture, but now that I think about it, as inactive as the fish were, it was more like looking at a color transparency, a still life in water. Seeing fish always excites me, even if they are sleeping, so I grabbed the pole and started jigging again. I maneuvered the jig so it was right in front of a perch's mouth and I even tried snagging him, but... I could see it wasn't a day to be fishing, so I quit one more time and looking down became the whole the reason for being there. The lake floor was covered with short weed growth and sticks scattered in a haphazard pattern. Up towards the river a tree that must have floated in during a spring melt-off, had sunk and was now half-buried in bottom muck.

When you're looking down a hole cut in the ice, the thicker the ice the narrower your viewing area, like looking through a telephoto lens on a camera. The thinner the ice the wider the viewing area, like looking through a wide-angle camera lens. Since I had cut a larger-than-usual hole, I could see a circle close to fifty feet across.

Suddenly out of the corner of my eye, I caught a glimpse of something brown in the distance, coming from the center of the lake, moving like a torpedo and heading toward the hole. I rolled out of the way just as an otter came up through the hole. An otter! The only one I've seen outside of a zoo. It took a deep breath, gave a look of thanks for drilling the hole that saved its life, slid back down the hole and disappeared.

Thirty Bucks

Exeter, New Hampshire is an old town by American standards. The Exeter academy was founded in 1777 (or the Year One, using the American calendar.) The Exeter River flows through the middle of town where it is so wide that it appears to be a small lake. This February the ice is still about fifteen inches thick, and, as the fog begins to part, a fishing village of several hundred fishouses becomes visible.

The Atlantic tides run up the Exeter past Portsmouth and on through Great Bay right into town where they still have enough surge to raise the fishouses as much as eight feet. Since the tide changes constantly, the ice along the shore is always cracking and heaving and never has a chance to re-freeze. Someone has put up a bridge to get across this area of unstable ice. It's a foot-wide board with wooden cleats nailed down as steps, and when the tide is out and the angle is steep, it's a little precarious. With an armload of gear and a couple of five-gallon buckets it's like walking a tightrope.

Ice fishing is a lot different here in Exeter than it is in the Midwest. These people aren't fishing for anything substantial like a walleye, northern or trout but rather for a diminutive silverside called a smelt, a fish that is used for bait in other parts of the country. The fishouses are called "bobs," lightweights that can be pulled around by one person. Exeter fishermen don't drill round holes but cut rectangular trenches all along one inside wall of their bobhouses. Over the trench there is a rod suspended like the one that holds the hangers in your closet. The spools for fish line are jammed onto the rod at given intervals so that when the rod turns, all the spools turn at the same time. The fishing is done with a small piece of worm and a bobber about a half-inch round that looks like the end of a thread spool. The smelt are so small that they don't even pull the bobbers down when they bite. The bobber just starts wandering around in the trench, so it takes some experience to read the bobber.

Another thing different here is that the fishermen keep their heaters on so high that the ice inside the bobs slowly melts. The fishermen here say, "The holes eat themselves out." Just before the ice gets totally unsafe, they move the structure to a new location. Walking around through this city-on-ice is not easy, because there are holes the size of fishouses everywhere. These holes freeze, but in February, when the weather is warm, the ice freezes just enough so you can't see the holes but not enough to make them safe to walk on. The fisherman who moves his house is supposed to mark the old location with stakes to keep people from falling through, but since wooden stakes aren't native to the ice, some fishermen just "borrow" the stakes from an old hole. In the warmer weather, then, you have a maze of unmarked, half-frozen traps on the ice which, for an out-of-state ice-wimp, can be a scary proposition.

Chris Cook, our main New England ice fishing informant, used to be the director of the Addison Museum of American Art in Andover, Massachusetts. Larry's first major national show was at Chris's museum, and they have been friends ever since. Chris is a fisherman but not an ice fisherman. He is also the kind of guy who can't get by a yard sale, a "free puppy" sign, a flea market, or a "boat for sale" sign without stopping. He is a nut for junk and a sucker for a bargain. This time it was a "for sale" sign on a fishhouse that stopped him. It was the first thing that caught his eye after he had "walked the plank" down onto the ice on the Exeter River.

Actually the sign read, "Open House." There were three guys jammed into the fishhouse, and they all got out so that Chris could look inside. It was a rather ordinary bob with a door, a window, a roof and four plywood walls. It wasn't fancy, but it wasn't ugly, either. It was the kind of structure that wouldn't end up on the cover of an ice fishing book, but, on the other hand, it was also the kind of place you could leave it next to your garage all summer without the neighbors calling the police. The most startling thing about it was that it was only thirty dollars. Being practical-minded New Englanders, the owners were selling it so they wouldn't have to dismantle it and haul it off the ice. They hadn't caught a fish in six weeks, and this seemed like as good a time as any to kick the fishing habit.

The guy in the bob next door had heard the owners warming up their sales pitch and he poked his head out to tell Chris, "Thirty bucks? It would cost a couple hundred dollars to build one like it." Chris didn't need anyone to tell him about bargains. He had a garage full of them. The only thing that kept him from plunking down his thirty dollars in the first two minutes was the fact that he was not an ice fisherman.

"Thirty bucks and it's yours. It's a pretty nice shack too. I'm going skiing. I'm giving up fishing."

Chris said, "You can't buy anything anymore for thirty bucks."

The guy who was giving the sales pitch was so wound up that he didn't notice that Chris was already sold on the deal. "It comes apart easily since it is made with nuts and bolts and separate panels."

"Yes, you wouldn't even need a truck," said Chris.

"It's also got an automatic bottom-finder."

"Wow," said Chris.

The guy had developed the closet-rod fishing system to an art, and it was all part of the thirty-dollar deal. When fishing smelt, you want to keep the hook and bait about a foot from the bottom. But since the tide is constantly moving in and out causing the ice and the shack to go up and down, the bobber has to be reset to keep the bait at the right depth. This guy had rigged a rope wrapped around the rod with an anchor on one end which sat on the bottom. The other end had a counter-weight which hung in the air inside the shack above the ice and below the rod. Each time the ice moved up or down, the weight would go up or down, and as it did it would turn the rod. The reels would turn also and they would reel the lines up or down to keep the baits at the same relationship to the bottom.

"I've got to think about it," said Chris, and he walked off into the ice fishing village.

These fishhouses were much smaller than in the Midwest where the ice is thicker and holds more weight. The thirty-buck special weighed only 120 pounds compared to 6,000 pounds for a typical insulated and furnished four-hole palace on Mille Lacs in Minnesota. Most of them appeared to have runners fastened to the sides, so all you had to do was tip them over, hook up a rope and pull them like sleds to the closest boat ramp.

Chris came up to a guy who was just pulling his house off the ice.

"They're selling that house for thirty dollars; do you believe that?"

"It's crazy. People are crazy. They don't know what it is to build a house."

Chris pointed out that it came apart, that it was all bolted together. The guy said, "Yeah. It's a good house. It's dumb that it's so cheap. It's dumb that nobody is buying it. Come October, they could get a hundred for it."

Chris said, "Thirty bucks. I could scratch his name off and put mine on it. I don't know where I would put it at home though."

"You should buy it."

"How's the fishing been?" asked Chris.

"I think it has been better down at Butterfield. It was good here for four days in December and now for two months it stinks."

"Well, if I bought this house I would have to get it off the ice, and I would also have to think about getting interested in ice fishing."

"Yeah, it wouldn't be worth much if you didn't go ice fishing."

Chris walked a little farther out and there were two houses half-sunk in the water; a third one had only its roof showing. Obviously these ice holes had "eaten themselves out" before their owners could move the houses. Two guys were fishing nearby in a house made of plastic-wrapped Styrofoam. When Chris stuck his head inside to talk he saw that the inside walls were lined with empty beer cans. These guys also had the only fish he had seen all day: a seven-inch smelt swimming in a bucket. Chris noticed a long black transmission oil funnel stuck in the wall with the big end inside and the tube end going out and emptying onto the ice.

"What the hell is that?"

"It's our pee-shooter."

The catheterized fishouse

One guy was wearing a red wool hunting cap with the ear flaps tied up. He got a bite while Chris was standing there.

"That was a Chinook salmon," he said.

Chris asked him how he could tell, and he said he couldn't explain it but there was a certain way they took the bait.

"There's a house back there for thirty bucks," Chris said.

"It's the wrong time of year to be buying a house," the guy with the cap said.

"It's a pretty nice little house."

"Maybe we ought to buy it," the other guy said.

"What are we going to do with it?" the guy with the cap asked.

"You can't have too many bobs," the other guy said.

"Well, I was thinking of getting it myself," Chris said as if he was afraid of losing it to these guys. "Something like this comes up and you can't believe you can buy it for thirty bucks, and it's an incredible buy. It's worth five times that. It is a nicely-made house, but the esthetics are unappealing. I can see that it would be fun to go out there on a cold night. I had a bunch of ice fishing equipment once, but I gave it all away. It was a monkey off my back."

"I don't know what to tell you mister," the guy with the red hat said.

"Tell him about the guy we threw into the drink for stealing those stakes," the other guy said.

"Yeah, there was this guy who stole the stakes off a hole and we came walking along..."

But Chris had already started back toward the thirty-buck fishhouse. By the time he got there the "Open House" sign was down and the owners had gone. He realized that he was more relieved than disappointed. It had been a narrow escape. The guys with the Styrofoam bob would probably get it. What the hell, it would be more healthy for them than sitting in plastic, and the esthetics of the plywood could still beat the tar out of Styrofoam, shrink-wrap and empty beer cans.

All the comforts of home

It doesn't get much better than this

Maine Trout

Here's another story from Lou, the guy with his own fishing museum and shop in Reading, Massachusetts.

I've been ice fishing for about forty-five years. I caught my best fish at Moosehead Lake. The year was 19... Let's see, my daughter was born in '63. It must have been 1964. Moosehead is the largest lake in Maine, in fact in New England. It's forty-six miles long and fourteen to sixteen miles across. You could put two Winnipesaukees in it. We were up there one winter fishing for what the Indians call a togue. It's what we call a lake trout.

We had over four feet of ice, which is common for Maine, and I had to go through it with a chisel. I tell you it was one hell of a lot of work. I cut two holes, set up my tip-up, lowered the bait down the first one and went back to set up the second one. While I was getting the second tip-up together, the first one popped up and I couldn't believe it. We were using jack smelt. That's what we like to use when we can find it. I pulled the line in and the smelt was gone, so I baited up and put it back down. I got back to the second hole to finish setting it up. I was sounding the hole so I wasn't there another two or three minutes and the first one went up again. Each time it went off none of the line ran out. You know, usually when a lake trout hits, it will make a run. I use a button to mark the line. When I find the depth of the water, I slide a button on the line right where the line comes off the spool. If the button goes down, I can tell how much line has gone out. It also gets me back to the same place each time. So the button had barely moved but the smelt was gone. This happened four times.

I didn't know what the hell was going on. You know how you go, "Aha, I'll get that so-and-so next time." I couldn't wait for the flag in the first hole to go up again. When it did, my friend yelled, "It's up again!" and I said, "Yeah, yeah, yeah." I just stood there and watched that hole for ten minutes and then I went over to it. Now we use big spools up there and thank God we do. When a big trout takes the bait you can hear them running, and as I got closer to the hole I could hear the spool underneath the ice going *dit, dit, dit, dit, dit* ... and I got over there and I looked down the hole and this great big spool might have had thirty feet left on it. This sucker has gone, *zoom*, you know, taking off for Canada.

Usually what you do when you get a laker, and by now I'm real sure it **is** a laker, is you let 'im make that first run. They stop. They turn around. They always take the bait headfirst. When he's making that run, you don't set your line. You'll yank it right out of his mouth. You wait until he turns around and swallows it. That's when you nail 'im. Well this thing had gone out so far, I said, 'I don't stand a chance,' and *poom*, I nailed him. Well, I never caught a twenty-six-pound fish in my life that gave me a pull like that. I've caught stripers in the thirty- and forty-pound range that didn't give me a hit like this. I think the most fun with lake trout is that they are heavy fish and they don't really give you a good fight until they see the boat. In this case it wasn't a boat that started his run, but the hole I had cut in the ice. When this son of a gun came up and saw the hole he took off again and you wouldn't believe the run. It took me thirty-five or forty minutes to get him up through the ice. You ask me if I remember him? I can still see him coming up through that hole.

Since they can't get cable TV, maybe next year they'll get a satellite dish

Deadfish Lake

The fishing trip was to a lake in New Hampshire which my hosts arbitrarily decided would be called Deadfish Lake. This was their favorite ice fishing lake, and there was no way they wanted me telling the rest of the country about it. So it's Deadfish Lake, and I hope we don't get any letters telling us that this is not the lake that these guys fish in, or complaints from New Hampshirites who know every lake in the state and never heard of Deadfish, or letters telling us that nobody has ever caught anything in Deadfish Lake because even in a wet year it never holds more than six inches of water.

Chris, my friend in Andover, had arranged this trip to Deadfish, and on our way we stopped in Concord to hook up with his friend Paul, Paul's son-in-law Brandin and Paul's fishing buddies Herb and Ted. We drove on in the dark through the mountains of New Hampshire on winding county roads. They didn't have to worry about me ever finding this place on my own, because I was lost in the first two miles.

Deadfish was set in the mountains and surrounded by snow-covered trees. It looked like the December picture on a nature calendar. There were only a couple of boarded up summer cottages on the south side and a nearly defunct summer camp set back above the road. There were four bobhouses placed artistically about the ice, one right where my guides wanted to fish. A plowed road led us right to the fishing area.

The road was in its spring mode, and we were walking on slick, clear ice. It was like the lakes I had been on in upstate New York where the snow had thawed and left a layer of water and slush on top of the ice. Another freeze had created a two-inch crust of ice on top of the water, and it was this thin top layer that we walked on. This time we didn't fall through into the slush, but the ice cracked and pinged and echoed off the forest as we trudged out to the middle of the lake.

When we got out by that first bobhouse, we unpacked the fishing gear. Paul had pulled all of his stuff on a plastic sled: his power auger, fishing buckets and extra gas. Herb, Chris and Ted carried large pack-baskets on their backs with the lunch and all the tip-ups. I had my red and white plastic Igloo cooler filled with a camera, film, a tape recorder and tapes.

In New Hampshire, each fisherman is allowed to use six tip-ups, so the six of us could drill thirty-six holes and put out thirty-six units. Once we got the tip-ups assembled, the hooks baited and the depths set, we stood around and waited for the action.

We listened to the wind blow and made small talk, since not much was happening. I thought maybe the fishing had never been good for any of the people I had interviewed. Maybe they were only telling the old tribal fish stories over and over. Maybe none of them really caught any fish. Maybe all the stories about how good the fishing was a week ago or a month ago were told to impress me.

Eventually we caught enough one to two pound perch and pickerel to keep us from getting discouraged, but it was definitely a low-key fishing day. The sun was out, and it probably warmed up to thirty degrees. The wind came through the pass between the two mountains in the west and there were times when it seemed pretty cold. They said it was one of the coldest spots in the state and even though it felt chilly, I figured this was just another fish story. It's not so much that fisherman lie; it's just that they exaggerate. I had traveled all over the northern states talking to ice fishermen, and everywhere I went I was told it was either the coldest or the driest or the wettest or the windiest or the spot that got the most snow on Thursdays in the whole country.

We were all standing there around the first holes. There hadn't been a flag for ten minutes, and it was too early to think about eating lunch, so Herb started a story that went like this:

"Paul and I and our wives make several annual trips together. Our favorite is the trip to Paul's lake cottage in Maine. There are only six cottages on the whole lake, so Paul thinks of it as his own private lake. On one of our trips there, I caught a four pound brook trout and I was so excited that I called Paul down to the lake so I could show it off. He picked it up, looked at it and then dropped it back down the hole. I couldn't believe it. He said, 'Yes, this is going to be a wonderful fish some day.'"

Paul let Herb finish and then he said to me, "Part of that story is true. I did let Herb's brook trout go. But it was maybe two pounds at the most. I'm not saying he's a liar. If it had been my fish that someone let go, I would have remembered it as a four-pounder, too."

Herb said, "That's why Paul let it go, so there wouldn't be any evidence that anyone else had caught a bigger fish in 'his lake.'"

In the next fishing lull, Paul told about the annual ice fishing trip that Paul's family, Herb's family and some other families take to Frogleg Lake in Vermont. "We were all drinking Bloody Marys and grilling food and fishing and partying and having a good time even though the fishing wasn't great. Herb and I decided to go to Gooseneck Lake only about ten miles away. We drilled our holes, set up our tip-ups and started feeling real thirsty. We talked about going back to Frogleg for refills on the Bloody Marys. We knew it was illegal to leave the lines unattended, but since neither of us had ever been checked by a game warden in our long fishing careers and since we were coming right back, we took off for drinks. Meanwhile, back at Frogleg, the game warden stopped by and checked everyone. Knowing that neither of us would do anything to break the law, they told the warden to hassle us just for fun. As we were heading into Frogleg we passed the warden just leaving for Gooseneck. Before we could even get our drinks we got the news that the warden would probably be waiting for us when we returned. With an *Ah, shit,* we ran to the car and drove back to the lake to find the warden waiting for us.

"I didn't have my Vermont license with me, and the warden was nice enough to let me drive back to Frogleg to get it. While I was gone, Herb turned on the charm and worked on the warden and the trainee who was with him. Herb's a good talker and he figured that the conversation was going real well. He had them laughing and he just knew he and I would get a lecture and a pardon.

"When I returned, Herb winked at me, and I knew that everything was okay, but then, when it was time for the warden to leave, he pulled out his summons book and wrote us up. Herb says we were summoned not because he had failed to talk our way out of it, but because the warden had to impress his trainee with the impartiality of the law and the righteousness of the game warden credo. Herb and I each lost our Vermont fishing licenses for a year."

After Paul's story, we ate the great lunch that Chris had packed: pita bread and crab salad. Feeling very full and satisfied, I walked over to the shore and lay down on a bare spot on the cold ground in the warm sun behind some wind-sheltering trees, and I slept while the fish did the same.

When I woke up, I asked Herb if he was sure the brook trout was four pounds. He said it was absolutely and without a doubt four pounds and by now it had probably grown to gargantuan proportions.

While I was talking with Chris another flag went up; it was one of the holes that was farthest out, and they gave me the minnow bucket and sent me over to catch the fish. "Catch the fish, Larry," they chorused. I missed it. It had taken out a lot of line and there was a beard of weeds on the bare hook. I baited it and looked around. Another flag shot up, about twenty feet away, so I went over there, took off a small perch, baited that hook and reset the unit. By then, the first tip-up I had set up only three minutes before was flagging me again. Before I got back to that one, the one I had caught the perch on went off. Chris came over to help me. He reeled in the line on the first one to find that the bait had been stripped again and there was nothing on the hook but weeds. Some good action, but not many fish.

So what do you do when you don't catch fish? You tell stories of course. Paul began: "Art was out in a boat fishing with some guys up in Maine. They were a long way from home when they began to run out of gas. The engine started coughing and missing while the bow waves were cresting over the windshield and coming right in the boat. Art found a bottle of Canadian Club in the boat, and he poured some into the gas tank and shook it a little and on they went. He added a little more each time the engine sputtered and finally they made it home with just enough booze left for everyone to have a shot..."

Stories are the back-up for poor fishing. Stories make us laugh and forget about being hungry and cold. Stories make us look forward to the next outing even though this one is not over yet. Stories make other people think what we do is great fun and it makes them feel bad they can't join us. Stories turn regular guys like Art into heroes.

What stories are lurking within this ready-made fishhouse?

Hook, Line and Hookers

We had been digging into this ice fishing story for only a short time when we first heard about another recreation that supposedly flourished on the northern ice. Actually what we heard was another variation on the theme of "I heard it from a friend who heard it from another friend whose brother's friend heard it at a bar."

The version of the story that we first heard was that there was a ring of hookers operating out of one of the resorts at Mille Lacs. No one we talked to claimed to know anything firsthand, but some of them had heard the same story we had heard. The Iceman said that a resort on Mille Lacs had gone under because of the ring, but he didn't tell us which one, and he didn't want to talk about it because the whole thing was bad for business.

We visited the *Mille Lacs Messenger* in Isle, Minnesota, which someone told us was the town Garrison Keillor had used as a basis for his Lake Woebegone stories (another unsubstantiated rumor.) At the *Messenger* we dug up a piece by Jerry Anderson from the winter of '87/'88, a response to a piece in the *Minneapolis Star Tribune* on the phantasmic Mille Lacs Hookers. Anderson said he had heard the stories of "The Ladies of the Lake" since the 1960s and even admitted that he would have liked to see one though he wasn't sure that he'd be able to tell them apart from the men, as bundled up as you have to get to stay alive on Frostbite Flats. Now Anderson doesn't come right out and say there is nothing going on; he just says he doesn't know anyone who will verify it. So we can still believe if we want to.

Maybe the story of "The Hookers of Frostbite Flats" was just another in the locals' repertoire of ice fishing jokes and stories. However, local business people who hoped to promote the image of Mille Lacs as a family recreation area were wishing it would go away. It was bad enough when the story broke in the *Tribune*, but then the wire services picked it up and Paul Harvey sunk his teeth into it and handed it back coated with moral fervor and disbelief. Paul Harvey, for crying out loud, right there with his hand on the heartbeat of America. Decent people all over the country believe what Paul Harvey says; it takes a real commentator to elevate rumor to folklore.

The funny thing was that the *Tribune* story even admitted that it was all just speculation. "Have you ever seen one of these ladies of the night?" "Nope." "Do you think they're really out there?" "Maybe." Nobody had been arrested. Nobody admitted to being a hooker. Nobody admitted to being a "customer." Right there in the *Tribune* article, Jim Forbord, state conservation officer who has worked Frostbite Flats for nine years, is quoted as saying that couples and fathers with their sons outnumber the all-male party houses. It was one of those where-there-is-smoke-there-is-fire stories. The writer creates the smoke and you fill in the fire.

Forbord had gone on to say, "Fishermen like to talk a pretty good brag. When you spend all weekend staring at a bobber, you start thinking about something else to do." And there we are back in fantasy land.

We heard about a lake in Michigan where the same activities had supposedly taken place, and another story about a pink house on the middle of White Bear Lake, but we'll let someone else look into those. Obviously anything you can do in the back seat of a car can be done more comfortably in the cozy privacy of a fishhouse on an icebound lake. And who's to say that someone doesn't get paid to spend the night once in awhile? The knocking on your door in the evening doesn't necessarily have to be the game warden checking for undersized walleyes.

Not much room, but it's portable

Moving Day in the Apostle Islands

I couldn't believe that a lake as big as Lake Superior would freeze enough so that people could actually walk on it, so I drove up to Chequamegon Bay in Wisconsin to check it out.

It was true: I found winter fishermen who go after perch and lake trout. Some of the trout villages are so far out you can't even see them from shore. However, there was lots of visible activity on the ice as I pulled into Ashland. Hundreds of people were clustered together, but I didn't see any fishouses. As I got closer I realized that the people were arranged in a big circle around a plowed race track. It could have been snowmobile racing, local stock cars or even the Chequamegon Bay 500.

From the shore at the boat landing near Ashland the fishouses looked like Indian teepees or A-frames, but they turned out to be canvas pyramid-shaped tents. I watched one guy struggling to set his up. "I made this myself, but I can never remember how it goes together."

Another guy inside a pointed tent was fishing for perch. They hadn't been biting for over a month, he said. "The fish are probably on a diet, and when they start biting they'll all be too skinny to keep. I'd really like to be another mile out there catching some lake trout."

I looked out where he pointed to the trout spot and got the shivers. It was more than two miles across open ice. No roads, no defined tracks. Not a comfortable place.

Driving out of Ashland up the west side of the bay, I came to the town of Washburn. Out on the ice the houses all appeared to be made of metal. One house was made entirely of used printing plates stapled to a wooden frame. Inside there was a man who was fishing for splake, a hybrid trout that is a cross between a brook trout and a lake trout. In his fish bag he had three beautiful fish. The man said that he got the printing plates for free. "They're not the most rugged thing, but they're nice and light and they make the house easy to move."

The man was a lawyer (the kind that practices law, not the kind that wraps itself around your arm.) He was involved in the case of the house that fell through the ice in the waters between Bayfield and Madeline Island in the winter of 1978. Bayfield is the next town north of Washburn where you catch the ferry for Madeline, largest of the Apostle Islands.

In Bayfield, the Pier Restaurant has a bulletin board filled with pictures of this extraordinary event. This was not a case in which someone lost a *fishouse*. This was a 1,000-square-foot A-frame house complete with a truck-tractor and huge tandem-axle trailer that had been carrying it.

The lawyer said, "There's a fine picture of the truck sitting on the bottom of the lake. It says, 'Dale Movers, World's Finest House Movers.' And there are pictures of the house. They took it across on wheels, and one set of wheels broke through. Part of the house went through the ice too, and it just kind of hung there until someone came up with the notion that since they couldn't raise it up they would sink it on down. I guess they actually went in the house and put sand bags in it. They thought they could sink it through and then salvage it in the spring. Well, in the going through, it broke up and the DNR said, 'You can't leave that thing in there,' so they had to get it back up and they just destroyed the thing in the process.

"I was hired by the salvager who was trying to get the huge truck out of the water. It was just a fiasco. It happened in about a hundred or a hundred and fifty feet of water. I won't swear to it, but it seems to me that the guys who were moving the house had just bought three of these A-frame things that a bank had foreclosed on. The bank sold them cheap enough so that these guys thought it would be profitable to move them out to Madeline Island. The first one made it out there. The second one fell through and the third one they left behind. It was right around the Christmas holidays. Everybody got stiffed, you know. The people who bought the house were suing Dale Movers. I don't know if Dale Movers was suing anybody. My guy was suing Dale Movers to recover his costs for removing his semitrailer from the lake. It was just a mess. And all the old timers were gabbing about it; they said that they had told the guy 'you gotta move it on skids;' the skids would have spread the weight out better. But they put it up on a few sets of tandem axles like you see when they move a house on land. They probably would have made it the other way."

No Fish in Okoboji

Larry drove down to Spirit Lake and Lake Okoboji in Iowa. On the way he went through Fairmont, Minnesota, read the sign "Fairmont Minnesota: City of Lakes," and was surprised when he couldn't find a single lake. He was also surprised when he got into Iowa and drove past Spirit Lake and there weren't any fishhouses. Okoboji was a different story. It had lots of them.

When I got to Lake Okoboji, I could see fishermen out on the ice wearing short-sleeved shirts. I walked out and talked to the two guys closest to me, sitting in their fishhouse with the door open. I got the usual story about how the fishing had been great until about two weeks earlier and lousy ever since. I told them the Minnesota fishing was just as bad. The short, talkative guy told me that he just got back from Lake Winnibigoshish in Minnesota and he had taken out tons of perch. He'd also made his annual trip to Lake of the Woods and this year it wasn't so good. He usually takes home about fifty walleyes and this year he only got to take his limit. I felt sorry for him.

Today they had been fishing on Okoboji since sunup and they had nothing to show for their time. They had seen a large walleye swim by, but it seemed to be wise to their tricks. I wondered if maybe they hadn't been seeing the results of overfishing, but I didn't say anything. I asked why Spirit Lake had seemed deserted, and they told me that the lake had swallowed a bunch of pickups the week before. Since then I guess everyone had gotten smart. I asked them if anything exciting ever happens on Iowa lakes other than people riding their pickups to the bottom or big fish swimming by and giving them the middle fin.

The short fellow answered, "There is the big house on the south side of the Clear Lake which has a felt-topped, eight-sided, regulation-size poker table. I was there once and I didn't even see any fishing holes in the floor. When I left, I was totally broke; these guys were professionals. I also know that some of the guys from around here have their fishhouses fixed up real nice on the inside to impress the girls." He turned to his fishing partner and asked, "Do you remember Tim Kaufman? I haven't seen him around for years. He did all right in his fishhouse."

"Yeah, and he didn't even fish. I'll bet he didn't obey the 'don't-lock-your-door' law. Just between you and me and the fish that aren't biting, it would take a real hard-ass warden to give a guy a ticket for having some fun, you know."

They told me that one fishhouse on the lake is called The Condo and it holds ten people and two kegs of beer, or nine people and three kegs of beer. It is in Smith Bay, so I got them to give me directions over there. There were supposedly fifty or sixty fishhouses there. I asked why and they said it was just a place that had a lot of shacks.

I got lost on the way to Smith Bay and I'm sure I ended up in some other bay, because there weren't many fishhouses there. I drove out to within two hundred feet of a very impressive pressure ridge. The ice was grumbling and shifting and making loud pops and pings as I walked over the pressure ridge. I kept glancing back at the pickup, worried that it might disappear and leave nothing but a big hole in the ice. I wondered who would drive it home if I were the one to go through the ice.

One nice fishhouse appeared to have been made from a plastic septic tank. Nobody was home at the septic tank, so I took a picture of it, tiptoed back over the pressure ridge, got in the pickup and drove to New York.

...and in the summertime, you can lay it on its side and play a marathon game of checkers

Honest as the Day is Long

There is another way to ice fish: spear fishing in a darkhouse, a fishouse without windows. During the daylight hours the sun shines through the ice outside the darkhouse. Just as the photographer looking through the view-finder of a camera can see better with a black hood over his head, the darkhouse fisherman looking down the hole in a clear lake can sometimes see the bottom thirty feet down.

The fisherman waits in the darkhouse with a spear in one hand and a string attached to a dangling decoy in the other. It looks like another fish, or a turtle or a frog or a crayfish or something else that's edible, and interesting enough to attract a hungry fish. One fisherman would regularly limit-out with large northerns using a muskrat decoy. Though spear fishing dates back to prehistoric times, the fish decoy appeared on the scene in the 1890s in the Alaska Eskimo communities, and soon after it appeared in the lower states.

Some decoys have become collectibles. The Museum of American Folk Art in New York City had an exhibition of fish decoys in February, 1990. On January 27th, 1990 a fish decoy made by Oscar Peterson of Cadillac, Michigan, was sold at auction for $18,700. Years ago Oscar traded his decoys for drinks and food and sold them for a couple bucks apiece. If you have one of his decoys lying around the house, even if it's one of his lesser creations, you might as well order that new car.

I heard about an ice fishing museum started by Jim and Mary Richards at Maplelag, their 440-acre cross-country ski resort in western Minnesota on the edge of the White Earth Indian Reservation just north of Detroit Lakes. I was told the Richards' decoy collection numbered around six hundred, so I made arrangements to go and chat with Jim about decoys and the museum.

When I left my home forty-five miles north of St. Paul at about four A.M., the weather was nice enough, but as I got close to Detroit Lakes, it started to snow and the closer I got to Maplelag the worse it got. I'll be damned if I'm going to drive over two hundred miles and then stop fifteen miles short of my goal, so I kept going. Everything was plowed, up to the last road, which had about fourteen inches of snow on it. I turned onto this road and kept my tires in the ruts made by other cars. I had gone about two miles when the tracks got abstract, and the snow rubbed against the bottom of my truck, slowing me down and making me spin out, ending crossways in the middle of the road. If the snowplow came through soon, it would have to take my truck along with the snow. Thanks to several of the Richards' neighbors, I finally made it to Maplelag.

After the usual formalities civilized people go through, I was viewing the Richards' decoy collection. Jim claims to have the best collection of Minnesota fish decoys in the country and I think he might be right. Like a kid bringing out all his toys to show the new kid on the block, Jim went through everything.

The first things he showed me were not decoys, but decorative fish carved by a man from Park Rapids, who was a poacher and apparently not a good one, because he spent his winters in jail carving fish. There was a brook trout, a rainbow trout, a lake trout, a brown trout and a walleye.

Next I saw a 1940 ivory-laced fish-stick made by a Minnesota Norwegian who had also made the birch bark frog lamp in the Richards' living room.

The first fish decoy he showed me was made by Otto Faue, a famous decoy maker who worked in the 30s in Buffalo, Minnesota. Jim says Otto and his brother Bill made the best fish decoys in the whole world. Some were realistic and some were impressionistic, but all of their decoys were painted well. They even painted the fins and tails, something most decoy makers didn't do. These decoys were made for spear fishing and traded for drinks in bars.

I asked his criteria for collecting decoys and I learned that some decoys are made by fisherman for fishing, some are made as works of "art" for display only and others are forgeries of old-master decoys made to fool collectors. Decoys made for fishing only are considered by Jim to be "honest" folk art. He doesn't collect the "art" decoys, because the line between the "art" and the "fake" is too thin.

"There's a Finlander in central Minnesota who makes decoys. He's an incredible artist who's made a hundred grand in the last two years making and selling decoys. He makes them look like antiques. They're too expensive to go in the water. They're great fish, they look ancient and they're very imaginative, but they are fakes. They end up in shops in the east selling for $100-$125."

I suggested this artist sign the decoys and they wouldn't be fakes anymore.

"Yes, that would solve the problem, but if he did sign them, they wouldn't sell as well, because people buy them thinking they're valuable antiques, not because they're art. This maker even copies the Minnesota masters".

I suggested he isn't making art if he's duplicating other artist's decoys.

"True, but he's making some originals, like this pregnant perch, not copying any decoy maker. Fakes are everywhere. When Oscar Peterson died, he had about five hundred blanks. Someone got them and painted them, so there are a lot of fake Oscar Petersons out there. Oscar was an artist, a folk artist, but his fish decoys were made for fishing."

The next decoy was a Thompson. It was real heavy, because it had a lot of lead in it. The ones with the most lead can be worked better in the water. This decoy was a $10,000 fish. Jim keeps his Thompsons in a safe-deposit box, but he got this one out to show me.

I couldn't figure out how he could look at two different decoys and tell they were made by the same decoy maker, so I asked, "How do you associate a decoy with the correct maker?"

"Each maker used different eye-tacks or buttons or paint. The device called the line-tie, the place where the line connects to the decoy, is different for each maker. The fin structure varies and there are other details. It's easy after a while."

He was showing me what he called the "creamers:" the very best. He showed me a little metal fishhouse which he said was folk art at its best.

I asked about his museum. "I'm just going to build a museum.

Folk art at its finest

Going to be on the property, attached to the lodge. Have fishing stuff like decoys, just the folk art decoys...maybe some spear houses and anything to do with spearing like homemade spears."

He was getting wound up and the decoys were coming at me faster than I could look at them. "Here's a decoy of an eelpout. Here's a sunfish. Here are some doubleheaders. This is a tripleheader, and these are called cigars, 'cause they're so thin."

I was still confused about fake decoys, so I asked if the fakes are easy to detect.

"No! No! Hard! You want to see a fake, here's a fake. Look at the rust, it looks like it's ancient, but it's only a week old. Everything about it is too good; it's too good to be true. It looks old. If you saw it in a flea market you'd say 'that's a great fish.' It's not honest, yet the maker is such an incredible artist."

He showed me two more fish decoys, one made as a work of art and one made for spearing. I liked them both and thought they were both works of art.

"Well, they're art, yeah! But one is not an honest, functional fish decoy. There's a difference between honest folk art and art. I like an old honest fish that has been in the water, not on some mantel piece." He showed me a couple hundred more decoys including a wooden eelpout and two trout with wooden tails and a very decorative one by an unknown maker.

I asked where he found all the fish in his collection.

"Have you heard of pickers? They go knocking door-to-door all through Minnesota. Three years ago there were five guys who went to every door in the state. Some doors have been knocked on five times. They knew I collect, so they came right here to me and I bought the cream of the crop. The fakes started two years ago and I haven't bought a fish since."

He showed me a crayfish decoy, some frog decoys, some turtles and a very large and heavy muskrat. Jim opened the Kimball book, a guide to ice fishing decoys, to a page showing a mouse, a baby duck and a salamander.

We looked at the foundation for the museum, part of an addition being built on the side of the lodge. In the lodge dining room, fish decoys were stuffed in the rafters.

"Oh yeah, they're everywhere. These were used this year. They were made by a carver on the Iron Range and because they're being used they're honest fish."

On the way back to the house, he told me that for years he collected decoys by an unknown maker. He figured they had to have been made in the St. Cloud area, so he put an ad in the St. Cloud newspaper.

About twenty leads turned up nothing. Finally he heard from a guy who said his neighbor used to make fish like that and the daughter was still living in the area. Jim visited the daughter who took him back to the shop where her dad had worked fifty years earlier. Everything was set up as if the man was still alive and working: the paint, a copy of a 1938 newspaper article on him, a board with samples of his six different models. Jim has all that stuff in his collection now and Schultz is not an unknown any more.

Before I left, he brought out the rest of the collection. Some had flecks on them. One looked almost ceramic; one actually was ceramic. One was so exquisite it reminded me of one of those Ukrainian Easter eggs. He had four more boxes of decoys including one made out of an insulator from an electric pole. Last was a sunfish by an unknown maker: "Real nice. Honest as the day is long."

A mess of decoys from the Richards collection

Used printing plates make for inexpensive and lightweight siding

A Pentagon, a Whale, a Peach Crate, a Black Lab and Jaws

We found Jeff sitting with his hand-built, wooden garden furniture at his place on the way to the town of Luck, Wisconsin. It was easy to find him because of the signs he had posted at every turn directing potential customers to his yard sale. Jeff said he was a carpenter and that one of his first building projects had been a fishhouse.

When I was a kid, my first fishhouse was a five-sided job that I purchased for seventy dollars. I bought it with money I'd saved from working on a farm. It was really a nice shack - everything came apart and it was only seven pieces. We sat around on benches. In the center of the wooden floor was a five-sided hole, and I usually punched two holes through the ice. It was small, but for a kid it was really fun.

We didn't have much money, so we used to take bean cans, cut half of them down, shape little handles out of the rolled tin and put a lamp or a candle in there so we could see what we were doing. We kept these lamps sitting down by the hole on the ice.

I had a wood stove so we could catch the fish and eat them right there. After school, I'd ask the bus driver to drop me off at the lake, and I'd go out there and fish until 9:00 at night. One evening we were catching crappies, and this friend of mine brought a crappie up and it bumped the candle holder so it fell down the hole. We kind of laughed about it and set out another one and that was that. About a week later, I was out there again with another friend, who must have been fishing right on the bottom because he hooked onto this tin can lamp, and, as he pulled it in, it propelled itself just like a fish.

I had no idea that it was the lamp, you know. And when he had pulled it right up to the ice, it wouldn't come through the hole. He told me to just stick my hand in after it. "Well, what if it's a northern? I don't want to get bit." We didn't know what to do about this big fish that wouldn't come through the hole. My friend was sure we could land it if we just got the head started through straight.

Finally we reached down and got it out. We sat and laughed. We'd really thought we had a whale.

I've had a lot of fishhouses since that pentagon. About eight years ago down at Deer Lake I had an 8x8-foot place. There were three of us fishing, and the water was so clear that we could see the fish down below; some really nice crappies were swimming by. They wouldn't take anything, bait, jigs, you name it, so I came up with this great idea to shut all the windows and make the shack dark, so we could see down in the water. I took a tip-up with a three-barbed hook on it, and

I started snagging fish. These crappies would go by and I'd drop that bare hook down under them and jerk up and snag them. Gee, before long I had four or five of these three-quarter to one-pound crappies. We were in there laughing about it, you know, and I never thought about what we were doing. I was just catching them and throwing them outside without realizing that no one else on the lake was catching crappies. All of a sudden the door goes *BOOM!* and there stands Wagner, the game warden.

All I could think was, "I'm dead meat now," because snagging fish is illegal, you know. So I stood up real quick. What I had done was put the tip-up in the corner of the house way up in the ceiling rafters and run the bare line down through my hands. So I stood up to hide the tip-up. Actually what saved us was that it was dark in there, and the warden's eyes took a while to adjust. I couldn't find my fishing license and he wanted a fishing license for everybody. I was so rattled that I couldn't remember if I had taken mine with me. Well, my uncle didn't even have one. He was sitting there and the warden asked him to pull up the line to see what he was using. And my uncle said, "It's not my pole. I'm just visiting." If he had touched it he would have been fishing.

Finally we got the warden, probably the worst one in this area, out of my shack. And we got by with it.

Another time we were fishing on Long Lake over by Centeria. We had these big fancy snowmobiles back then, and we had tip-ups strewn all over the lake. While we were sitting on our sleds, out comes this old beat up '59 or '60 Nash Rambler driving across the lake. And we all looked at this car like we couldn't believe it was still running. This old guy gets out and he's all crippled up. He hobbles around and looks at the ice. He just stands there right in front of us. We're kind of looking at each other and winking by now, and the old man is looking around. We figured out that he was looking for some holes that were already dug because he didn't feel like digging any new ones. We're watching him, you know, with all our fancy equipment, waiting for a flag from one our tip-ups.

Anyhow, the old guy opens up the trunk of the car and he lifts out this wooden peach crate. And he goes over and kicks the ice off the hole he has chosen and sets the peach crate there. And we're kind of snickering as he goes back to the car and opens the back door. He's got one of those old steel bait-casting rods that are about five feet long with one of those casting reels that backlashes all the time. And he hooks on a big sucker minnow and drops the minnow down the hole. We are all watching every move. He ties a red handkerchief on the line and he sets the pole on this box. And we're laughing by now. We can't believe what we're seeing. The old-timer turns around and starts walking back to the car, but he barely has changed direction before the handkerchief goes *spuuuuu*, right down in the water.

I bet you it was a fifteen pound northern he caught. We're sitting here with all this sophisticated equipment and he comes out with a peach crate and a two-dollar outfit and it was just a fantastic northern. We were sick. He got up and put all his gear back in his car and down the road he went. He had his fish, and we never caught a thing that whole day.

Once, on a Super Bowl Sunday, I'd punched the fishing holes and set up a little table in a corner of the fishhouse for the TV. I had the jumper cables coming off the battery in my truck outside against the shack. People I'd never seen before were fishing all around us.

My friends and I got the lines squared away, and we turned on the TV. We were sitting there drinking pop and nibbling on our munchies, you know, watching the game with our bobbers in the water, having a good time. Pretty soon I could hear these auging noises. These people outside were drilling holes all the way around my fishhouse so they could listen to the game while they were fishing. I was afraid they were going to drill up all the ice around the shack and we'd fall through.

There were six or eight guys who had drilled holes right up next to the shack, and they would come in and warm up and check the game and the munchies. It turned into quite a party.

I had a good spearing experience up in Northern Minnesota. They put little shacks on the ice up there, cut square holes in the center of the shack and spear northerns through them. The hole is probably 3x3 or 4x4 and they sit on benches around the inside of the house with these spears.

They use a decoy, like a fishing lure without the hooks. This draws the big fish in and they spear them. There was a group of houses in a bay. This guy was in one of the houses spearing, and he was jigging his decoy around trying to attract a fish. He had his big black lab with him, and he was jigging away and a northern came up into view and the dog saw this big fish and dove in after it. The dog's down there and they were wondering if he was in trouble. But all of a sudden he came up in one of the neighboring shacks. This other guy's sitting there and here comes this black lab through the water and up through the hole. They said the guy went right through the wall. He was so scared he didn't realize what it was.

If you'd come ten years from now you'd be getting the stories from my son Michael. He's ten and he's already designed a jig and caught a pound and a half crappie on it. He's a pretty good fisherman.

When Michael was only three, we were fishing on Deer Lake and had moved our shack out to a drop-off because there were some nice perch out there. Michael wasn't into fishing yet, so he was just watching. My friend punched out the floor holes and I got the holes drilled and cleaned out and the lines baited and set.

My friend and his son and Michael and I sat down in a row on our buckets, and we were talking with our lines sitting there and all of a sudden I heard this *click*. I looked down and my fishing pole was gone. Deer Lake is real clear and I could see my rod just slowly going down through the water. I couldn't reach it. Michael came over and looked down the hole. He just couldn't believe a fish could be big enough to do that, you know. Pretty soon we were all laughing about it, and I rigged up another pole and put the line in and we sat back again. Not more than two minutes later, I hear this *click, click*, and I look up again and my second pole is going down the hole. I grabbed it and I felt the fish, but it let go and I got that pole back. My son came over and looked down the hole and said, "That's it. We going home. Jaws's down there."

There is sometimes more down there than meets the eye

Orville's Oldsmobile

Orville was as much a part of Center City as Enoch's Bait Shop at the Conoco station. He never married, and he never fell in love that anyone knew about. The closest he came to expressing affection was for his 1962 Oldsmobile. He bought it brand-new, washed it every weekend and waxed it once a month in fair weather. In the winter he left it in the barn and rode everywhere with his son Leland.

Every Thursday night Orville stopped for a beer at the Trail's End at the north end of town. He talked to his sister Beth and asked after the kids, drank his beer, and used the toilet. One Thursday night he stepped into the empty parking area in front of the bar and his car was gone. It had simply disappeared. No one had heard it start and no one had seen it go.

"Hippies," Beth said.

"What?"

"It was hippies that took your car. I seen 'em here a few days ago just looking over the place."

There were no police in town, and he had to wait in the bar for the state highway patrol to come, ask him questions, write down the license and take his description. It took a long time to get all the information because Orville wanted to tell them the whole story of how he had saved his money and how he had chosen an Oldsmobile in the first place.

It was two months before anyone saw the car again. Some campers at Coon Lake called the game warden to report seeing a family camping in Orville's Oldsmobile. The warden called the police, but by the time they got out to the campground at the lake, there was no sign of Orville's car.

The kids went back to school, football season came and went, and Orville continued to mourn his car. The lake froze up in November and the first fishing holes appeared in the ice. By the middle of December the first pickup trucks were out and a couple of fishhouses from town were in place.

Walter Matson, the game warden, was the one who finally found the car. "It was the week before Christmas, and I was out on Coon. There were quite a few fishermen out and twenty or thirty houses. I saw this old Oldsmobile, though it was so muddy and dented that I didn't really recognize it as Orville's. I watched for awhile and I realized that no one was fishing near it, so I went to check it out. Someone had been fishing from inside the car, using it as a fishhouse; the whole front seat was filled with beer cans and the back seat was taken out and a hole drilled through the floor. It was all gutted out and it smelled terrible. The engine was gone and we had to tow it off the lake. We never found the people who stole it or the people who dragged it out there, and as far as I know no one ever told Orville that it went to the junk lot. He loved that car, and he wouldn't have wanted to hear what really happened to it."

Larry's Fishouse

It would be difficult for someone to go out on the ice three winters in a row interviewing ice fishers without wanting to get involved, so Larry hired an architect to design a fishouse which he plans to build and use one of these upcoming winters. It's hypothetical. It's a dream. It's a fantasy. It may be that his banker won't want to hold a mortgage on a fishouse. If it is built, it may never get used and it could end up in the yard like his canoe which only gets moved when the lawn gets cut. It could fill up with rags and aluminum cans and discarded fishing poles and broken snow blowers.

Everyone who thinks about fishouses has a favorite style. Some like big fancy ones with four fireplaces and some like little cubes to curl up in all day. Some fishouses are decorated, some are utilitarian, and some are gaudy. When I think about having a fishouse, I think about one that will stand out on a crowded lake, one that will make me famous. My fishouse will be built from the plans by St. Paul architect Peter Carlsen, and it will look like a lunar landing module. It will grab the eye of anyone looking across the lake. Tour buses will drive by and people will talk about it.

It will be just like home, only more compact. It will have a frying pan and a sauce pan, some nice-looking plastic dishes and extra silverware in case anything drops down the fishing hole. There'll be food staples like candy bars, beer nuts, taco chips and coffee. Sleeping gear will be a borrowed sleeping bag, a pillow and an extra blanket; extra clothes will include long underwear, another coat and a spare pair of boots. It will have Rolaids or Tums, foot powder, chewable vitamin C, a tooth brush, aspirin and a chemical toilet.

For entertaining guests I can get by with a deck of cards and a good supply of pop and beer. For the grandkids some crayons and coloring books will do. I'll want my *National Wildlife* and my copy of *A River Runs Through It*, and a good road atlas to plan a trip to some warm place. I'll have several pairs of reading glasses even though it will be harder to lose them in a fishouse. No television, but a radio and a tape player with my favorite tapes will keep me from getting bored when I'm tired of reading.

People go to their fishouses to get away from the pressures of home and work and telephones and such. Not me. I will give up the answering machine, but I will have a cellular phone, so I can have a perch pizza delivered now and then. I will have my computer to write letters and keep my journal. I'll see if the mailman will deliver my mail to the fishouse.

I'll choose a lake next to some town, so I can walk over and get my laundry done every once in a while and drop off the trash and I'll go to the store for supplies.

Perch pizza? Perch? Fish? I hadn't thought about that. I suppose, as long as I'm going to be out there for ten weeks, I might as well do some fishing. I don't think it's the law or anything, but I would look silly out there if I weren't fishing. That means I'll need some equipment. Stuff like a tip-up unit, an ice auger, a jigging stick, a box full of tackle, a minnow bucket filled with minnows and a fillet knife. A rattle reel would be most convenient. If I can get the fishouse in an area where there aren't too many fish, fishing wouldn't take up too much of my time. I wouldn't want this fishing thing to get out of control.

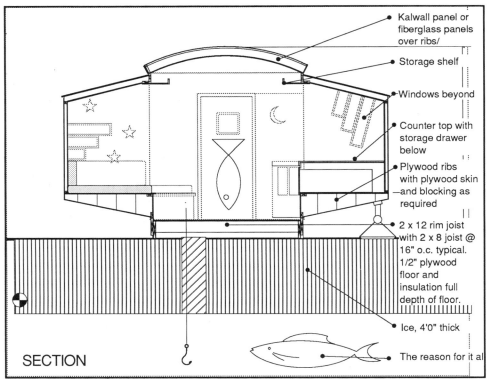

Kalwall panel or fiberglass panels over ribs/

Storage shelf

Windows beyond

Counter top with storage drawer below

Plywood ribs with plywood skin —and blocking as required

2 x 12 rim joist with 2 x 8 joist @ 16" o.c. typical. 1/2" plywood floor and insulation full depth of floor.

Ice, 4'0" thick

The reason for it al

SECTION

"The Plans"

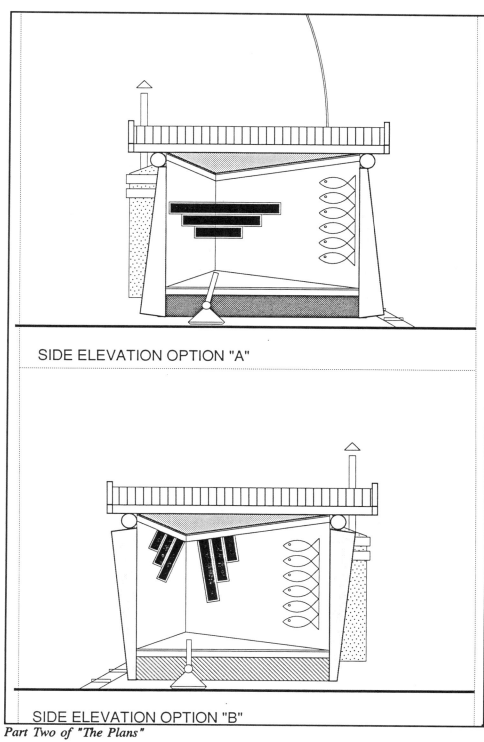

SIDE ELEVATION OPTION "A"

SIDE ELEVATION OPTION "B"

Part Two of "The Plans"

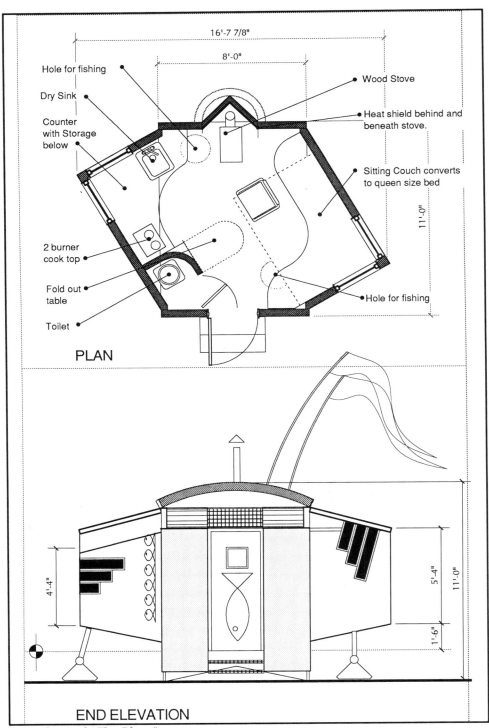

Hole for fishing

Dry Sink

Counter
with Storage
below

2 burner
cook top

Fold out
table

Toilet

Wood Stove

Heat shield behind and
beneath stove.

Sitting Couch converts
to queen size bed

Hole for fishing

16'-7 7/8"

8'-0"

11'-0"

PLAN

END ELEVATION

4'-4"

5'-4"

1'-6"

11'-0"

Part Three of "The Plans"

Nordic Teahouse

Whenever you buy something on sale and then brag about it, you know that someone is sure to tell you about a place where you could have gotten a better deal. The same thing happens when you finish a book. "A book about ice fishing? Did you get the story about the jet that crashed on the ice and the pilot who got out to fish before help arrived? Didn't I tell you how my mother-in-law fell in and got stuck in my fishing hole?" It was Gordon, our own publisher, who waited until the manuscript was in before he said, "Why didn't you interview the monk?" Hold the presses! What monk? Does he have a fishouse? Save space for one more chapter!

Brother Paul August Jasmer lives at St. John's Abbey in Collegeville, Minnesota, near St. Cloud. He calls his fishouse his hermitage. He has a license for it and even a hole cut in the floor for fishing. The license is required by the state, but the hole is just in case - just in case - there is a requirement that he fish. Brother Paul is not sure that he really needs the hole, but he is sure that he doesn't want to fish. His fishouse has become a winter retreat on the ice.

"My house provides a rustic haven on winter days and a place where I can read to the lulling crackle of the fire. In the environs of wind and snow, I read and study Old Norse/Icelandic literature, the sagas and histories written in Medieval Iceland, the land of fire and ice, volcanoes and glaciers. For me the image of fire and ice is replayed as the oranges, pinks and reds of the low winter sun are reflected in the glare of the ice."

In 1982 Brother Paul built his fishouse out of scrap wood from the lumber shed on the St. John's University campus. He assembled it in the woods behind the lumber yard along the west back-bay of Lake Sagatagan. (Lake Sag, as it is called, is the major water feature on the 2400-acre grounds purchased in 1856 with funds supplied by King Ludwig for the original monastery.) When the snow fell and the ice formed, Brother Paul put his shoulder to his newly-constructed house and discovered that it wouldn't budge. He had pictured pulling it out onto the ice with a rope like a big sled, but it was too heavy to move from the woods. Disappointed, Brother Paul abandoned his project for two years until he got the idea of using aluminum printing plates for siding. The idea came from his dad and the plates came from the print shop on campus. Paul removed the heavy wood exterior and fastened on the aluminum with screws and washers. The house was not as sturdy as it had been, but it was light enough for him to move. In fact, that first winter it was so light that a blizzard took it some hundred feet across the lake where it collided with a more permanent house. "My collision insurance refused to cover the mishap."

"A winter afternoon starts with a trip to the abbey's carpentry shop where I fill my sled with oak scraps for the wood-burning stove. I also stop at the kitchen and pick up my tea, water and Scottish shortbreads. At the fishhouse I get the fire started in the stove and set the water to boil. It has become a celebrated winter pastime for some people of the faculty, library and bookstore, ecumenical center and the monastery to venture out to my fishhouse for tea and conversation. I greet them with a hearty welcome, prepare the tea in a white and blue ceramic pot, and serve it on a linen-covered table set with china cups."

Brother Paul has a more sophisticated way of expressing himself

A visit to Brother Paul's is described in the abbey's in-house newsletter: "...Brother Paul hosts guests to enjoyment of a sunny January day, Queen Mary tea served in china cups, conversation and poetry (Nordic sagas, and winter poems by Robert Frost and Toshimi Horiuchi.) There was a bit of elegance, a bit of 'roughing it' in a wonderful escape from stuffy indoor winter air."

Brother Paul feels that being on the ice is being in the mystery, the border between the known and the unknown. When the walls are buffeted by a storm, you are isolated, warm and secure, but a little frightened. That's where mysticism is, right at the edge of this world. "The Irish hermits who went to Iceland - they wanted to be on the fringe of the unknown. That's where they found God.

"Winter is the most majestic time of the year...the winterscapes...the snowdrift sculpture...the sun glaring on the ice. That's why I wanted this fishouse to escape to. I notice that people are more open when they are out in the open. Nature enlivens people. I read an essay about the Swedes, that the fishermen do not go into the woods to get away from it all, but to extend it all. I believe that. That's what this fishouse is, that's what everyone's wilderness house should be.

"The first word in the rules of St. Benedict is 'listen.' That means to listen to what's going on around you. You can hear things when you are quiet out in the snow on the middle of a frozen lake. You are surrounded by an inexhaustible beauty of nature which enlivens you and enriches you in millions of ways."

Brother Paul and friends about to enjoy tea and conversation. Photo by Brother Paul Richards

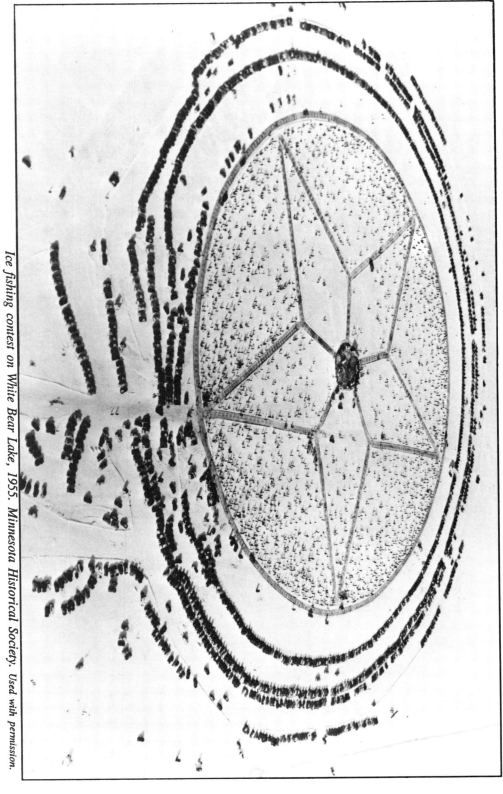

Ice fishing contest on White Bear Lake, 1955. Minnesota Historical Society. Used with permission.

Photo Glossary

Your personal visual guide to assorted, selected,
not necessarily all-inclusive ice fishing equipment.

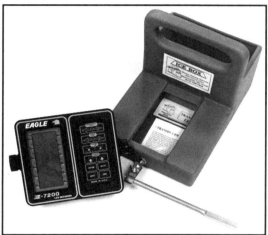

*Electronic gadgetry used to take a little of the
"luck" out of fishing*

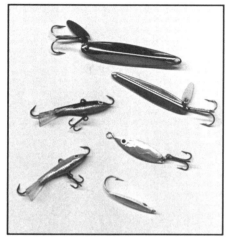

Assorted jigs for splake or trout

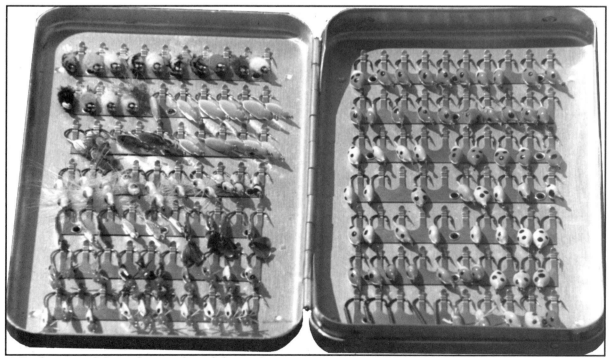

A jig for every lake and every day of the week

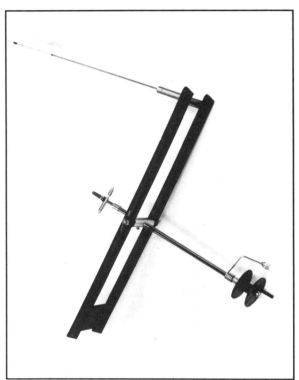

Sturdy steel tip-up designed for the career fisherman

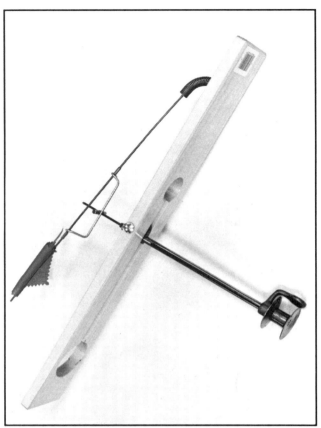

Typical wood-base tip-up; a little less costly

Yes, a rattle wheel

This must sell great: it's a "WALLEYE Wheel"

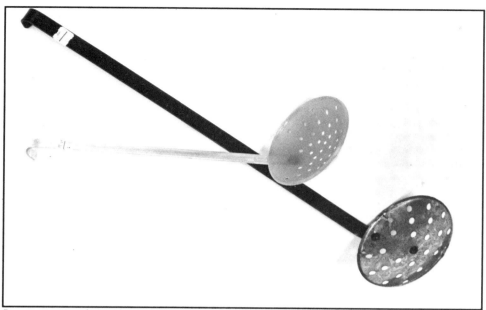

Ice scoops, to keep the hole clear

A mousetrap or set-up

Another type of set-up, or "cheater"

Your basic Swedish Pimple pole

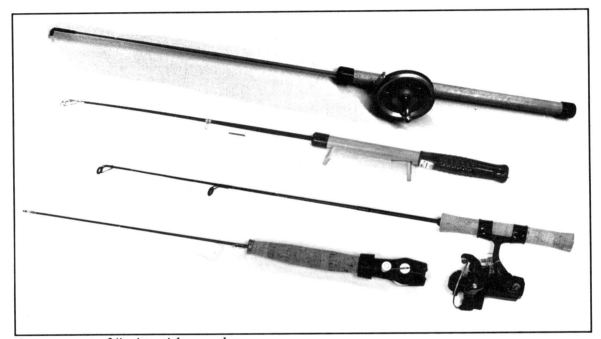
An assortment of jigging sticks or poles

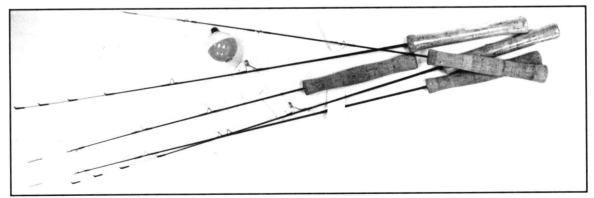
Even more jigging sticks

Equipment photos by Magnus Berglund

Glossary

Auger: A tool used to drill a fishing hole in the ice. Some augers are hand drills and some augers are gasoline-operated. Occasionally there will be one that's electric. Someone once said: "In order to drill a hole in the ice, you have to be smarter than the ice." That's why the auger was invented.

Bluegill: A freshwater member of the sunfish family which is bluish in color and has a dark-blue tab on its gills. Also called bream, or sunny.

Bob: To bob, the practice of bobbing; a fishing method invented in New England in the 1940s. The end of a girdle stay is fastened to the inside wall of an ice fishing shelter and a fishing line is attached to the other end. The other end of the fishing line has a hook and a heavy sinker attached to it. The fisherman twangs the girdle stay and the bait moves up and down for up to a minute at a time. This action attracts fish.

Bobber: A device used to notify a fisher that there is some action on the lower end of the fishing line. It usually floats on the top of the water, but there are some exceptions. (See "spring bobber" and "floating bobber.")

Bobhouse: The name used for ice fishing shelters in New England. Named after the practice of bobbing.

Bream: A northeastern nickname for any member of the sunfish family.

Brook trout: A member of the trout family. Also called brookie, native trout and speckled trout. A four-pound trout is a very good fish.

Burbot: A freshwater member of the cod family. Also called cusk, dogfish (though not a true dogfish,) eelpout, freshwater cod, gudgeon, lake lawyer, lawyer, ling, ling cod, maria, methy, mother eel, mud blower, pout and spineless catfish. It's a very slimy fish.

BWCA: Abbreviation for Boundary Waters Canoe Area. A national recreation area located along the Minnesota/Canada border. It is an area with many lakes connected by short stretches of rivers. The BWCA rules prohibit the use of all motors, engines, and other mechanical devices. A place where people go to paddle and portage all day long in the name of fun.

Chum: The equivalent of stacking the deck in the fisher's favor by scattering food in the area where the hook and bait is located, so as to attract fish and get them into a banquet mood.

Cisco: A member of the salmon family, whitefish group. Also called herring, lake herring (though not a member of the herring family,) and tullibee.

Crappie: A fish in the sunfish family. There are two kinds: the white crappie and the black crappie. They are also called speckled perch, speckled bass, speck, calico bass and good eating.

Darkhouse: A fishhouse without windows which is used for spearing fish. Also called a spearing hut.

Decoy: Fish decoy, that is. It is used in a darkhouse to attract spearable fish. Decoys are usually made to look something like small fish. They are also sometimes made to look like crayfish, frogs, mice, muskrat, turtles, baby ducks, salamanders, butterflies or giant marshmallows.

DNR: In some states, this is the abbreviation for Department of Natural Resources.

DNR Agent: Someone who works for the DNR, probably the game warden.

Eelpout: See "burbot."

Fish stick: An ice fishing pole. It has a place where the line is wound, a point so that it can be jabbed into the ice above the fishing hole and an eyelet on the other end for the line to go through.

Flag: Winter fishing gear used from a distance is equipped with some way of signaling the fisher when there is some action involving a fish. This signaling device is called a flag. Being flagged is the situation when the flag is sending its message to the fisher. Not to be confused with the man on Gull Lake in northern Minnesota who has a fishhouse with two flag poles. If the man flies one flag, the resort/bar on shore sends a meal out to him. If he flies the other flag, they send out a mixed drink. The reason he uses two flag poles instead of two different-colored flags, is that he sometimes wants to order both a drink and meal.

Floating bobber: A piece of girdle stay attached to the end of a fishing pole in such a way that one end touches the pole and the other end is away from the pole. When a fish tugs at the bait, the fisher will know there is a "bite," because both ends will be touching the pole.

Girdle stay: A piece of spring steel that was formerly a functional part of a girdle.

Ice chisel: A tool used to chop holes in the ice. Also used by someone walking on thin ice to tap the ice before stepping on it to see if it is safe. It has pretty much been replaced by the auger.

Ice scoop: A tool used to remove residue ice or snow from a fishing hole that has recently been augured. It is also used to chop and remove new ice as it forms on a fishing hole which is being used.

Jack: See "northern."

Jig: A type of ice fishing lure that is moved up and down to attract fish. It is used bare or with bait such as a minnow, leech or grub.

Jigging stick: A short rod with or without a reel used to move a bare hook or a baited hook up and down in the water to trick a fish into trying to eat the hook.

Killing fish: The term used for catching lots and lots of fish. Even in "catch and release," the term applies.

Lake trout: A member of the salmon family. Also called laker, mackinaw, gray trout and togue. The world record is sixty-five pounds, but a ten-pounder is a good one.

Lawyer: See "burbot."

Limit-out: To catch the legal daily limit (and maybe more) of any species of fish.

Minnow: The minnow and carp family are a combined family of fish. In the US and Canada there are over two hundred species in this family. Some of the smaller species are used as fishing bait.

Minnow bucket: A compartment or container to keep minnows in until they are used as bait.

Mille Lacs: The name of one of the biggest lakes in Minnesota where the "de luxe fishhouse" first appeared. There are an estimated 5,000 fishhouses on this lake each winter. The resorts on the shores of the lake rent fishhouses, plow the roads on the ice and offer many other services to fishers.

Mousetrap: A device used in ice fishing that holds the fishing line so as to keep the hook and bait in place. It automatically releases the line when a fish takes the bait so the fish can run with it. Sometimes referred to as a set-up. It is called a "cheater" when used illegally.

Northern: A member of the pike family. Also called jack, jack fish, gator, great northern, northern pike, pike, snake. A small one is called a hammer-handle. Not to be confused with a pickerel which shares some of the same names.

Panfish: A fish small enough to fit uncut in a frying pan. It is usually a member of the sunfish family, but it can also be a perch.

Perch: A family of fish including sauger, yellow perch and walleye. Common name for yellow perch. Also called 'poich' in the eastern US.

Pickerel: A member of the pike family. Also goes by most of the names used for the northern. There are two kinds of pickerel, the chain and the redfin. Both are found only in the eastern US and Canada.

Pressure ridge: A line of heaved, cracked ice which is higher than the ice around it. For a better description, see the chapter called "The Iceman."

Poich eye: The eye of a perch as said by a New Englander. Used on a jig or a bare hook, it is good bait for catching other perch and/or other members of the sunfish family.

Pour House: Name of a bar in Siren, Wisconsin.

Pumpkinseed: A member of the sunfish family. It is dark green on its back, gold-yellow on its belly and it has a distinct deep gold to orange chest.

Rapala: A brand name for a widely-used jigging lure.

Rattle reel: A fishing reel that attaches to the inside wall of a fishhouse. The line unwinds and goes straight down into the fishing hole. When a fish bites the hook, the line starts to unravel from the reel, so that the bells inside the reel fall around and *ding-a-ling*. There are high-tech AC and DC electric variations of this gizmo.

Scooper: See "ice scoop."

Set-up: See "mousetrap."

Smelt: A family of fish. They average seven inches in length. They are either eaten or used as bait.

Snake: See "northern."

Spearing hut: A fishhouse without windows used for spearing fish. Also called a darkhouse.

Splake: A hybrid member of the salmon family created by fertilizing the eggs of a lake trout with the milt of a brook trout. First developed in the 1880s.

Spring bobber: See "floating bobber."

Spud: See "ice chisel."

Sunfish: A family of fish including the black bass, bluegill, crappie, pumpkinseed and sunfish.

Sunnies: More than one sunny.

Sunny: Midwest name for any fish in the sunfish family.

Swedish Pimple: A brand name for a jigging lure. The company also makes other ice fishing equipment.

Tip-up: The fishing pole that a fisher sets up outside the fishing shelter. It's a self-contained fishing unit that signals the fisher if and when there is possible action on the line. When the fish messes with the bait, a flag (usually red) goes up and the fisher goes to this device to (hopefully) collect the catch.

Togue: See "lake trout."

Tullabee: A member of the salmon family, whitefish group. Also called cisco, herring, lake herring (though not a member of the herring family.)

Walleye: Member of the perch family; also called walleyed pike (though not a member of the pike family.) These fish are in high demand for eating. Fishermen have been known to lie, cheat and dynamite to get one.

Bibliography

MacLean, Norman, *A River Runs Through It*, University of Chicago Press, Chicago, 1989.

Kimball, Art, Brad and Scott, *The Fish Decoy*, Aardvark Publications, Boulder Junction, WI, 1986.

Becker, George C., *Fishes of Wisconsin*, University of Wisconsin Press, Madison, 1983.

Sternberg, Dick, *Freshwater Gamefish of North America*, DeCosse, Minnetonka, MN 1987.